Big Hands Big Heart

Big Hands Big Heart

Sport Media

This book is dedicated to Eric Senior and Veronica, my dad and mum, on behalf of the five grateful brothers who they brought into the world and gave the best possible start in life.

Eric Nixon

Published in hardback in Great Britain in 2012.
Published and produced by: Trinity Mirror Sport Media,
PO Box 48, Old Hall Street, Liverpool L69 3EB.

ISBN: 9781908695147

Photographs/images: Trinity Mirror/Liverpool Daily Post & Echo, Press Association Images, Eric Nixon collection.
Every effort has been made to obtain the necessary permissions withreference to illustrative copyright material.
Any oversight will be rectified at the earliest available opportunity.

Printed and bound by CPI Group (UK) Ltd, Croydon, CR0 4YY

CONTENTS

THANKS, FROM ERIC...

This book will make it clear how much my family and friends mean to me, and I would like to acknowledge them at the start.

Rachel is the wonderful lady who shares my life, along with her daughter, Amy. Eric, Jessica and Bradley, my three children, are simply the best. I am so proud of them and love them to bits.

My eldest brother, Alan, is a fantastic father to his own kids and has three sons, Gary, Lee and Gabriel, as well as one daughter, Ashley, and a grandson, Romeo, who is Gary's lad. Alan has honesty and reliability in spadefuls and is always willing to do things for other people. Like me, he moved to the Wirral and now works as a driving instructor round the highways and byways! Leslie, the hard, committed footballer who always loved a battle, has a wife, Jackie, and three sons – Justin, Daniel and Jack. He is very much the family man, a quiet and unassuming type, who gets on with life his own way and if you want help he's there for you. Philip will also do anything for you and wants nothing back for it, just as mum and dad would have wished it to be. Jason, the youngest, is a proud husband and father with a wife, Jill, and sons, Troy and Beau.

Rachel's family have been a wonderful help over years. Sincere thanks to her mum, Cynthia, her dad, Peter, and sister, Jane. Without them, we would have been in some very difficult situations and, believe me, you find out who your real friends are when you are out of the spotlight and everyone thinks that as an ex-professional everything is rosy in your garden.

Dave 'Taffy' Jones went out of his way to encourage me in the early days and never doubted that I would turn professional, even when I was beginning to have second thoughts. He would take me into the open area behind his garden and we would practise for hours. He would slate me at times but it had the desired effect, and I could not have got where I have today without the help of Dave, his wife Jan, and his family.

Thanks also to Dave and Thelma Robinson, not forgetting their dog Alfie. Dave and Thelma have been brilliant over the years. Both he and I have had our fair share of bad luck and we have always provided a shoulder for each other to lean on.

Keith Nethercott is another pal who I owe a lot to and he and his partner, Kate Grattan, are close friends. Ged Wells is a respected figure in the Liverpool area, and we have been friends for about 15 years. Ged has played a lot of charity games with me and devoted many hours to working for good causes. A special mention should also go to his wife, Mandy.

Rachel and I are forever grateful to Jan and Mandy Molby, both for their friendship and also the work that they do for the Claire House Children's Hospice on the Wirral.

My thanks, also, goes to John Aldridge for agreeing to write the foreword. John and his wife, Joan, are two of our closest friends and we have shared many happy times. A special mention should go to John's late father, Bill, who I always got on well with.

My sincere appreciation goes to Trinity Mirror Sport Media, not only for their support in publishing the book, but also throughout my career. When I became only the third Tranmere winner of the prestigious Liverpool Echo Dixie Dean award, given for services to football on Merseyside, it was one of my proudest moments in the game.

Finally, my special thanks go to David Mitchell, who has been patiently listening to me spouting on, and reproducing all the many Nico thoughts and opinions in written form.

Eric Nixon,
March 2012

FOREWORD BY JOHN ALDRIDGE

I arrived back on Merseyside in 1991, just after Eric had captained Tranmere to victory over Bolton in the play-offs at Wembley. I immediately recognised him from the shape of his arse, because I had seen it so many times as he bent over to pick the ball out of the net after I'd scored a goal against him! He was a massive figure, physically and otherwise, at Prenton Park and a top-class keeper. I used to call him 'England's Number One Nico'.

I know how honoured he was to be given the skipper's role by Johnny King, and he took the responsibility seriously. He went out of his way to give my family a warm reception on our return from Spain and I will always thank him for that. Behind the joker who thinks he is Elvis there is a genuine guy who is as loyal a friend as anyone could wish to have, and Joan and I are fortunate to count Eric and Rachel as two of our closest friends. Nico and I often have a quiet drink together on a Sunday night. Nothing on the lines of what he used to get up to, but a chance to reminisce over a pint or two and remember the great days and the fun times at Tranmere Rovers.

One of the things that binds us together is the passion that we showed for the game. This often spilled over and got us into trouble, and I well remember the rumpus that occurred in the tunnel after the home match against Norwich City. I was manager and Eric was coach at the time and tempers flared after we heard that one of the Norwich players had been bullying one of our guys. We decided to go for revenge, and both Eric and I were at the heart of the action!

Eric took his goalkeeping very seriously and was a big student of the game. He was excellent at throwing to feet and with out-and-out wingers of the quality of Johnny Morrissey and Pat Nevin, I was never short of opportunities. He was a reassuring presence at the back and you always knew he was there. My biggest issue with him concerned the Zenith Data classic against Newcastle United in 1991. The game will go down as one of the most memorable in Tranmere's history. It finished 6-6 after extra time, and we won on penalties. Big Eric saved two spot-kicks in the shoot-out and took the Man of the Match from me after I'd scored a hat-trick. I seem to remember he went home with a mountain bike for his heroics. The game had been live on television and I was gutted.

I had the highest regard for Eric as a goalkeeping coach and asked him to work with the keepers when I was manager at Tranmere. I was determined to build the best possible coaching base at Prenton Park and Eric worked with John Achterberg and Joe Murphy. John started the 1999/2000 season in tremendous form after a mediocre pre-season and he would be the first to acknowledge the tremendous help and encouragement that he received from Nico. You've got to be mentally and physically strong as a goalkeeper, and Eric tackled every aspect of the job with John and Joe and did a great job for me.

Everyone connected with Tranmere Rovers will be eternally grateful to the big man for the part that he has played in the club's success. It is a privilege to count Eric as a friend and I am delighted that he has been able to have an opportunity to tell his story – or as much as he can remember!

John Aldridge,
March 2012

A BIG CHARACTER

I first met Eric at Fleetwood Town Football Club. I had taken early retirement from education and was working for the press team. I had reached the exalted position of a seat on the team coach for some of the away games. Eric would get on with a lot of the players at the Windmill pub at Tabley, near Junction 19 on the M6.

He would immediately start the chat and the joshing, often from a seat next to his old Tranmere mate and Fleetwood Town manager, Micky Mellon. I sat nearby and would listen on as he dished the banter, cracked the jokes and poked fun at himself and others, always speaking ten to the dozen. He lightened the mood on many an away journey and the memories of a long career would flow. A big character physically – and his presence matched it.

One day he offered to make me a cup of coffee. The great Eric Nixon – a player I remembered clearly from the halcyon Tranmere days and on the telly – offering to make me a cuppa!

What a nice guy.

I was working on my laptop as he walked up the coach to do the honours. He returned minutes later, cup in hand.

Suddenly, there was a stumble and the cup was heading through the air towards me. I shot from the seat but there was nowhere to go – window on one side, person on the seat beside me on the other, table blocking my way ahead. The cup that landed on my laptop was empty, just as it had been when it left his large hand. I recovered from the panic and looked up to see a broad smile grinning down at me from the big man. Respect.

A further conversation after training one day revealed that big Eric was keen to write a book about his life. He had completed a few pages of notes but was finding it difficult. I offered to help and he said that he would e-mail me the stuff. It never arrived. Instead, voice recorder in hand, I accompanied him into a quiet room some days later, a bar ironically, and he started talking. Minutes into our first chat, he pulled off his top to reveal a huge picture of his beloved dad tattooed on to his left shoulder. From that moment on, I feel that I've known him all my life.

David Mitchell,
March 2012

Chapter One

A SECOND CHANCE

'As I stood up to get out of bed my left arm started feeling strange. Things were not right'

John Aldridge led Tranmere Rovers into the first full season of the new millennium. His team had ended the previous season 13th in Division One, a mid-table position that was becoming quite a habit as it was the fifth consecutive season that Rovers had finished comfortably placed, neither threatening promotion nor facing relegation. However, that consistency was about to change as the club entered what was to become a bizarre season which involved a memorable FA Cup run and massive problems in the league.

The cup campaign started with a long trip to Portsmouth in the third round. We had already had the league visit and lost 2-0, but goals from Steve Yates and Andy Parkinson booked our place in the fourth-round draw after Tranmere had come from behind to give Pompey their first home defeat since September. Fans and players crowded round the radios and televisions as the draw was made and we were given another away tie, this time at Everton. You can just imagine the excitement that caused on the Wirral. Aldo described it as the 'game of the round'. It was just the fourth time the two close neighbours had come together in a top-level competitive match, the last occasion being 33 years previously when Everton had won 2-0, also in the FA Cup. Here was a chance to earn some bragging rights and forget for the time being a disappointing league season which had included defeat in seven of our last 10 games.

It was January 2001. It was towards the end of my playing career, and I was also on the coaching staff at Tranmere by this stage. My preparation for the game had been affected by bouts of indigestion. I remember mentioning the problem to the club physio, my great mate Les Parry, in the week before the game but we shrugged it off. A fortnight earlier, we had been at an away match, at Bolton I think, and there were four of us in a group having a drink – me, Aldo, Les and Kevin Sheedy. Les still relates the story of how I went a funny colour on that occasion, and how I had to get outside for some fresh air. Something did not feel quite right.

The day before the Everton match, Tranmere coach Ray Mathias was taking a session with some of the younger players. I suggested that Les and I join in, one on each side. Ray agreed, but asked us to wait a couple of minutes. While we stood and watched, I told Les about chest pains that I was beginning to feel on my breast bone. He asked if I'd suffered a knock of any kind. Before I could answer, we were called on to the pitch. I think I scored five or six times, which wasn't unusual! However, I couldn't shake the problem off and it came back to give me some discomfort at our overnight hotel. Les and I were still talking about it on the bench at Goodison the next day. I told myself to stop whingeing and to get on with it.

Aldo had fancied his chances of creating an upset. We had a good record in cup competitions. We always worked hard and stuck to our game plans, while Everton were proving a little unpredictable at home. We were also guaranteed a good portion of the attendance, with over 6,000 fans making the short journey across the water. In fact, the kick-off was delayed by 15 minutes due to crowd congestion caused by ticket problems as a result of a postal strike in Liverpool.

Walter Smith fielded what looked like a strong side, and the atmosphere at kick-off was tremendous. To spice things up there was the return to Goodison of Paul Rideout, who scored the only goal for the Blues in their 1995 FA Cup final win over Manchester United and Peter Johnson, who had been Everton chairman but then left the club controversially to return to Tranmere, after previously moving the opposite way.

The match started off at a great lick, with Everton attacking the Gwladys Street. An early drive from Thomas Gravesen brought a superb save from John Achterberg, while Steve Watson blasted a shot just over. The first quarter of an hour was not easy, but we showed great character and got back into the game. The pace of Parkinson up front caused problems, and we were quicker to the ball in midfield.

It was soon first blood to us as Jason Koumas and Parkinson broke. Sean Flynn whipped in a cross towards Steve Yates, whose looping header at the back post fooled Thomas Myhre and crept inside the post. Suddenly, Everton had a mountain to climb. With increasing control of midfield, we went further ahead with a classy Koumas strike from the edge of the box. Everton duly left the pitch at half-time to a chorus of boos.

Walter Smith made changes at the break but they had little

effect. We put the game to bed when Yates headed home unmarked from a Koumas corner. Steve gained cult status at the club for his two-goal bonanza. In fact, I think the fans always call 27th January, the date of the match, 'St Yates' Day' in his honour! For the club, it was one of the proudest days in our history, with a heroes' reception from the fans as the Evertonians showed their disgust and anger at their team's sorry performance. The Blues faithful all went into hiding, with our fans' chants of 'Are you Chester in disguise?' ringing in their ears!

Despite all the Goodison excitement, I was still aware of my health and my condition continued to cause concern come Monday morning. As I stood up to get out of bed my left arm started feeling strange, and I suddenly felt that things were not right. I was just getting ready to go to training and phoned Les at about half-past eight.

I told him that the pain was now going down my arm. Knowing that these were classic heart attack symptoms, the sensitive side of Les came out and his reply was: 'Are you taking the piss, Nico?!' Nevertheless, he told me to get in straight away and he would get hold of the club doctor. As I drove in to the ground the pain was getting worse, so I phoned him again.

He asked where I was, which was on the Woodchurch, so he told me to go straight to Arrowe Park hospital just a few minutes away. By now, the adrenalin was beginning to kick in as I felt more pain.

At the hospital, I got behind a kid who must have been about eight years old. He had a cut across his head and was with his dad so I politely waited, even though I was all over the place. The lad's needs were more important than mine at the time. I finally talked to a nurse and within half-an-hour I was up in Ward 2 of the Coronary Care Unit on a drip! I had, indeed, suffered a heart attack.

It was a life-changing moment, and they say that at times like this you look back on your life. Well, it's true. I thought about the highlights of my career, what I had achieved in the game and how fortunate I had been to play 650 matches. I had played at the top level for Manchester City, the club I supported from childhood. This had included an appearance at Wembley, the famous stadium which I was privileged to visit on many more occasions with Tranmere Rovers. Not many can say that they have walked up the famous steps as the winning captain but I can. For three consecutive years I was selected for the PFA Team of the Season by my fellow professionals. I played against the top players and at the biggest stadiums across the country.

Rachel, my girlfriend at the time but eventually to be my wife, was contacted at Birkenhead Market, where she had been chatting with a mate of mine, Johnny Orr. She was panicking more than me by this stage, as I knew I was where I should be and getting the best care. The doctors decided to give me an angiogram, to see where the problem might be in the coronary arteries. They told me that news on the Friday ahead of the Monday and my first thought was that my childhood pal, Stewart Lynch, had died on the operating table during an angiogram just two months earlier. It was to be a long weekend.

The tests showed that my 'undertaker's artery' as they called it was 90% blocked, and I had only given myself a chance of survival by keeping fit. Before I knew it I was heading down the tunnel under the Mersey with flashing lights and a police escort. The next stop was Broadgreen Hospital across the river in Liverpool. There was no time to waste.

As I started the recovery, I was getting lots of concern shown from the football community. John Aldridge and Les Parry were regular visitors, but family considerations were complicated as arrangements had to be made for visits by both Karen, my ex-wife, who wanted to bring the children to see me, and Rachel, my current partner. As you can imagine, there was a press presence around the hospital and everyone saw Karen leaving and Rachel arriving. They did not realise that it had been carefully planned so that they did not bump into each other at any point! We needed to behave in an adult way rather than let differences of opinion get in the way.

The hereditary nature of the disease means that my kids will eventually have to be screened. Of the five brothers in my family, Philip and I were the ones to suffer. However, you just have to get on with it and I eventually returned to coaching at Prenton Park. Tranmere were brilliant, allowing me time off when I needed it. Coaching had never replaced playing but in my head I had come to terms with that and got on with it, grateful of the chance to continue making a contribution to the game following my operation. Little did I know that I would later be called back into action.

The cup heroics continued and did nothing for my dicky heart! The fifth round saw us back on the south coast where we earned a goalless draw at one of my old clubs, Premiership side, Southampton. It wasn't pretty but a job done. By the time we kicked off at Prenton Park in the replay, we knew the winners would face Liverpool at home in the quarter-finals. However, Aldo banned any talk of that possibility in the dressing room and around the ground! It was to be another of those memorable home occasions which will forever go down in Tranmere's history.

With Southampton 3-0 up at half-time, the commentators

were beginning to talk about the tie with Liverpool, while BBC radio even went to commentary from another game. What followed was one of the greatest comebacks in cup history. With the Saints thinking it was all over, the lads came back strongly. A hat-trick from another former Saint, Paul Rideout, left the game level with 10 minutes to go and the atmosphere was just crazy! Just when you thought it couldn't the tie went up another gear when substitute Stuart Barlow stuck home the fourth with about seven minutes to go.

We managed to get through an agonising final period when Southampton had another chance, and duly went through to the dream tie against the Reds. Liverpool manager, Gerard Houillier had described the performance against Southampton as of 'Champions League quality' and certainly had a few things to think about as he prepared his side for the short trip under the Mersey.

Liverpool had beaten my old club, Manchester City, in the previous round and we gave them too much defensively. Danny Murphy and Michael Owen put them up at the break and although we came back twice through that man Yates again and Wayne Allison, it was never enough. Steven Gerrard and Robbie Fowler from the penalty spot made the tie safe, and Liverpool went on to win the competition against Arsenal. It had been a disappointing end to the run, but the cup exploits that season will stay long in the memory for any Tranmere fan who watched them.

By that stage, Rovers were bottom of the table with 13 games left. This was an amazing situation to be in after all that had been achieved in the cup. We won only one more game and went back down to Division Two – bottom of the table with 38 points and just nine league wins. By that stage, my good mate, John Aldridge, had decided that enough was enough as a manager and resigned.

The season had been a turning point for both my club and for me. As it ended I knew that I was now going to be on medication for the rest of my life. My life had been put into perspective. My family and my health were my priorities. I had a lot to be grateful for in the game, as well as a loving and supportive family, and I did not want it all to end so early, as it had for my wonderful dad.

I was 38 years old, the same age as my dad had been when he had his heart attack. It was also the same time of the year. My dad, a smoker and drinker, did not survive but I had been given a second chance – and I was determined to take it.

Chapter Two

AN EARLY LOSS

'I remember standing and thinking, even at the age of seven, that everything was over'

I lost my dad to a heart attack when I was seven years old. Eric Nixon senior was 38 years old and had a lot of living left in him. Sadly, he was unable to shape my life in the way that he and I would have wanted. Dad was a massive United fan and used to get so upset when they lost. He would have loved to have watched my football career develop, although there would have been plenty of banter flying around when I signed for City. I often wonder what he would have said and felt every time I ran out with the Sky Blues and, particularly on those occasions when we played the Reds.

I think about him every day. My brothers and I have all moved on through our lives, and a lot of water has passed under the bridge. Indeed, I think all of us think about what might have been had 'Big Nico' not passed on when he did.

Dad died one night at home. My four brothers and I got up

for school the next day as normal and Uncle Walter, dad's brother, gathered us in our small kitchen and told us the news. We all stood there side by side like tin soldiers. There was Alan, Leslie, Philip, Jason and myself. The gas was lit on the stove and something was cooking.

We were too young to take in the news but I remember standing and thinking, even at the age of seven, that everything was over for me. Relatives and neighbours came round but we went to school as normal. My eldest brother, Alan, was the only one of us who went to the funeral. He remembers dropping the flowers into the grave the wrong way round but watching as they somehow turned and landed the right way on the brass plate that was attached to the coffin. Alan was 11 and like a father-figure to us, a role that he took very seriously.

Dad had been our rock. He was a hard-working, smoking, no-nonsense type of guy. A picture of a dapper-looking young man dressed to impress in dark suit and tie stands on top of the sideboard in mum's house. Was this really the same man who used to warm his big hands around his mug of tea each morning, then dunk his toast? It's funny what you remember. I would ask him why he did it and he always replied that it 'put hairs on your chest, son' – and he died of a heart attack!

Looking back, I find it very difficult to remember when my father was alive, and I cling on to the memories that I do have. I try to think of when we laughed, when we cried, when we played. I never had enough time with him, so the memories I have got I cherish to this day. I regularly visit his grave in the huge Southern Cemetery in Manchester. It's not far from the road and as I make the short number of steps from the car, my mind goes back to remember good times sadly ended all too early. I have my quiet times alone with him, and tell him what has been going on in my life. Sometimes I take my kids with me. I tell them about him. I show them the large tattoo of him that dominates my left shoulder, alongside the dates when he was born, and when he died.

Twenty-five years or so after his death, Alan and I had decided to put a new headstone on dad's grave, as we could not afford one at the time. The marker stone actually showed we had been visiting the wrong grave for all those years, and had been at that of a two-year old girl. Although it was an upsetting discovery, we decided not to take the issue any further.

It is only when I grew up and started to see my own kids develop – Eric Junior, Jessica and Bradley – that I began to understand what mum and dad did for us. He would have been able to follow the fortunes of 12 grandchildren and one great-grandchild had he lived, and how he would have loved to have spoilt them all.

It still upsets me to talk about dad today. He and mum gave me strength of character and an awareness of the importance of manners and respect. I owe it to them to try and pass that on to my own kids, and people around me. There is a lot of my dad in me and mum says that I am his walking double. Curiously, I was also to have a heart attack at the same age and in the same month as he did.

I was born on 4th October 1962 and, although I was too young to appreciate it at the time, my musical hero, Elvis Presley, was at the height of his power. The 'King' had four separate number one records in that year – 'Rock A Hula Baby', 'Good Luck Charm', 'She's Not You' and 'Return to Sender'. I'm sure my mum must have rocked the pram backwards and forwards as she hummed along to the great man and tried to get me to sleep. Mind you, she probably wouldn't have taken me out much in those early months as the winter ahead was the worst since 1947. It caused severe congestion of football fixtures which was a factor in my local team, Manchester City, being relegated from the First Division as Everton emerged as champions. Thirty-one points from 42 games was a poor return for the team which was to feature strongly in my career.

The other club close to my heart was mid-table in Division Four. Tranmere Rovers, under manager Dave Russell, also suffered weather-wise, having 14 games postponed between mid-December and the end of February 1963. I was blissfully unaware of all this as I lay warm and snug in my cot, being doted on by family and friends who referred to me as Robert!

Yes, believe it or not, I was called Robert David for a year. I was the third son of a third son and so was my dad so he decided to change my name to Eric, like his. It took him a year to work it out, mind. According to my mum, he changed it just in time because I was beginning to answer to the name Robert. My kids still don't believe to this day that I was originally given a different name but I have proof because the original names are on my birth certificate.

My brothers and I began life in Harpurhey in Manchester. Harpurhey is about three miles north-east of Manchester city centre. In 1830, someone described its many 'pleasant views'. By the time that I arrived in the world, that had all changed. It was an inner-city suburb surrounded on all sides by more inner-city suburbs such as Blackley, Crumpsall and Moston. I've always seen myself as a bit of an entertainer, and find it amusing that some of the best known figures connected with Harpurhey are performers.

Comedian Les Dawson worked as a butcher there before his career took off with 'Opportunity Knocks' in 1967. Meanwhile, Little and Large started their careers at Bernard Manning's Embassy Club, as did another comic duo Cannon and Ball, while Freddie Garrity (Freddie and the Dreamers) lived in Brewery Street.

We lived at 13 Shepley Street, and it was a hard upbringing. Not many were born with silver spoons in their mouths in that neck of the woods. We lived in a three-bedroom terrace house on a cobbled street, and we slept tops and tails. One of my earliest memories was of dad turning on the downstairs lights first thing in the morning and seeing the beetles scuttling for cover.

He would then kneel down and try to get the coal fire going. If it was a struggle he would put the shovel in front of it and hold a sheet of newspaper around it to get the flames going. I would see the bright orange light beginning to flicker on the other side of the paper and knew the fire was 'catching on'. We soon got used to life with an outside toilet and no bathroom.

There was no money for gas or electricity and we relied on second-hand boots and clothes. The telly was black and white and we had no idea what a duvet was. We were a backstreet gang. We'd chat with the rag and bone man and the McAlpine's guys who brought lemonade and dandelion and burdock to the door. We would watch the coal man deliver the bags and count them in to make sure there was the right number.

As you would expect, with five lads knocking about, there were many bumps and bruises. I still bear a scar on my head caused when Alan slipped and put my head through the window. Instead of leaving me there he dragged me back through! I must have been about 18 months old at the time. The house has been knocked down now but I still go back to the area. I revisit my past a lot, in fact, so much so that my wife and family get fed up about me going on about it. I'd love to have a chance on that programme, 'Who Do You Think You Are?'

I also remember us having a rented property in Moston. It was two-up, two-down but the people who had it wouldn't pay up so my dad suddenly had enough, marched round and told them to get out. They did, but not before setting the place on fire out of spite. My dad had to spend a part of every weekend for quite some time doing jobs there to get it back to shape.

Dad worked at the Dunlop's Rubber Factory and also had a job at the Forester's Arms on Rochdale Road. We did not have many aunties, uncles or grandparents to look after us. We got on great, though. Life was pretty simple and straightforward for the Nixons. There were few luxuries and no frills. We'd get the plastic ball out for a kick-about and when we burst it we mended it and started again.

Alan, being the eldest, remembers more than the rest of us including a trip we made to Tatton Park, a mansion with massive gardens near Knutsford in Cheshire. It was probably only about 20 miles or so but as we rarely left the street, this was like going to Cornwall. We went in two cars with another family from nearby and, on the way back, dad's brakes failed. We all had to come back in the other vehicle, a big estate car, and Alan clearly remembers us sitting on the bed crying our eyes out, hoping dad would get back alive.

Chapter Three

FAMILY VALUES

'I was the captain and expected to lead by example... but in that way I could not'

When I was four, we moved across Manchester to Withington. Number 3 Bosley Avenue was a council house like the one in Shepley Street, but a massive upgrade all the same. Alan often says that the move was the best thing we ever did as a family. The house is still there, less than a mile from my beloved Maine Road, and just off the main Princess Road which runs up into Manchester city centre from the M60. Mum now lives around the corner where she is regularly visited by not only five sons but 12 grandchildren and one great-grandchild, Romeo. I didn't remember much about the move at the time but I do know that we developed strong friendships and values for life in that part of Manchester.

Next door but one was the house belonging to Matty and Josie Lynch with their five lads and one daughter. Between the two families lived Maureen Waddington and her two daughters. All the lads would be in and out of each other's houses all the time. We were like 10 brothers. In fact, mum was so short-sighted she used to belt one or two of the Lynches, thinking they were us! We used to find any excuse to go to Josie's because she gave her lads a pudding after their dinner. My dad had moved job at Dunlop's and we thought it would give us a better way of life. He later worked for a subsidiary of Port Sunlight, the soap business, in Withington. I only found that out recently and took my mum round the Port Sunlight village on the Wirral thinking how strange it was that I lived nearby.

Dad worked long hours and either travelled by bus or walked. I didn't remember much about what he did because we just accepted that he went out every morning and came back later. He also worked nights and this meant that everything was left to mum. After he died, terrible though it was, nothing much seemed to change in the house because it was always mum around during the day, even when he was alive. Even though he grafted and put in the hours away from the house, we knew that he always cared and looked after us.

We made some fantastic lifelong friends in those days. They made growing up that much easier, and gave us a feeling of stability and security. Time moves on, though, and sadly a lot of those good mates from the streets of Withington are no longer with us. Terry Lynch was older than me, more Alan's age, and a diamond of a fella who followed my football career around the country. He never recovered from an industrial accident and died of pneumonia. I visited him in the funeral parlour, gave him a kiss and said goodbye to a great mate. Terry's brother, Stewart, was to die in hospital on an operating table. Then there was Shaun Mulcahey, whose coffin I remember helping to carry from his house to the church, through the streets. Pete Baynon, my best man when I married my first wife, and Alan Illingworth, are also no longer with us. I think about these guys all the time and it always brings back some great pictures of a happy childhood.

Some of my fondest memories are of Saturdays. After our usual trip to the pictures, the afternoons were always dominated by 'World of Sport' with Dickie Davies. It was one of the few times my dad spent with us and we used to fight him on the couch when the wrestling was on from five to four until the football results came in. We would be Big Daddy or Giant Haystacks or nasty, bad Mick McManus. You can imagine what that would have been like with five lads but dad always took it in good fun, like I do with mine. He loved the rough and tumble but, when needed, he also had a sensitive side and would be ready with a bit of TLC if you cut yourself or stubbed your toe on the pavement.

Dad used to love the war films on television. He would always kid us on that he had fought in the war and flew planes into enemy territory. He had loads of stories which made him every inch the war hero. We were impressionable kids who believed him, even though mum would always remind him that he had never actually left England. In these type of situations we saw dad at his best. He liked nothing better than to bond with the lads. It must have been a release for all the long, hard hours he worked to keep us all going.

When we did get quality time together he would take us to Wythenshawe Park, a beautiful piece of open parkland in south Manchester. It was only about three miles away down the Princess Parkway but, like the trip to Tatton Park from Harpurhey, it seemed more like 200 miles. In my years as a first-team player at Manchester City I had to run all the way back from the park to the training ground in Moss Side and I can tell you that there was never a time when I did not see my dad standing with us by the paddling pool, telling us about his days in the war and how many Germans he had shot before he went over and got the enemy to surrender all by himself.

When it came to running the house, which wasn't often, dad didn't have a clue. Mum was rarely away from home and held everything together but, on one occasion, she went into hospital for a hysterectomy operation and he was left in charge. He couldn't rely on his war record in that situation, and made some crazy decisions. Once, we asked for a drink of milk and he gave us a pint each! A pint – it was like Christmas! Maureen Waddington and Josie Lynch would have to come in from next door and help him out at times like that. They were fantastic neighbours, and were there for mum when dad died. In fact, everyone in the area looked out for her.

So far, I've concentrated on dad but, beside him all the way, was a remarkable woman. Veronica, my mum, was, and is, a very resolute lady. She had to be. A strapping young man was to leave her life all too early with five lads under the age of 12 to bring up and she in her mid-30s. You do not realise until much later, when you have your own kids, what mum must have gone through and sacrificed for us throughout the years that followed dad's death. Overnight, she had to be mother, father, confidante, shoulder to cry on – and much more besides.

My dad had a bit of a pension but not much, so mum had to make do. She could not go out and bring home a wage herself because she had to look after us. How she made do, heaven-only knows. I know that one way was to recycle our clothes from one brother to the next. With no income coming in for trackies, fancy trainers and the like we would rely on hand-me-downs passed through the brothers, according to age and height. Leslie used to get Alan's, I would get Leslie's, Philip would get mine and so on down. We would also get stuff from the Army and Navy stores. How bad is that? You try going to school dressed as a Japanese sniper! I suppose Alan came out of it best. As the oldest, he would get first dibs on new gear and we weren't half jealous of him.

There is no doubt that mum sacrificed a lot to be there for us, and it could have all gone wrong if she hadn't been as strong as she was. She could easily have settled for second best and just done enough to get by but, no, she looked after us, fed us regularly and brought us up to have respect and manners. We were always looked up to and respected, as we respected others. We never brought the police to her door. In fact, we were more scared of her than the cops. When we got a crack from mum, we felt it, believe me.

I remember one time she came in after being out at the pub with friends – which did not happen often at that time. We had played Alan up rotten. Having been brought up on beans on toast, sugar butties, dripping butties and homemade cakes, when our mum got the odd chance to go and socialise, and boy did she need to go out, Alan had the unenviable task of keeping a house full of testosterone-charged lads in check for the next four or five hours. On this particular occasion, she made us queue up at the side of the settee and wait for our punishment one-by-one. The snake belt came out and our asses were red raw for a week.

Mum had to be physically and mentally strong, and life must have been very hard for her. Her own childhood had been difficult. She came from a broken home and from the age of two spent six years in a Children's Cottage Home, which is now

Styal Prison. Her dad re-married but things didn't go smoothly and she finished up in a Dr. Barnardo's home in Ripon for six months, after which there was yet another move, this time to Lytham St. Annes on the Lancashire coast. The Lytham home closed soon after and she finished up in London, near Wembley Stadium. She remembers collecting at the ground for Dr. Barnardo's little knowing that, many years later, a son of hers would play at the famous stadium.

I think I managed to avoid feeling the weight of mum's hand until I was a teenager, when I started giving her a bit of lip. In fact, I think I was quite useful to her before then. I used to help her make the beds. I did it for ages, then one day it suddenly clicked that none of my brothers was offering so I gave up. I also spent some time re-planting and seeding the front garden at Bosley, until the lads ruined it by coming through the hedge on their bikes.

I was definitely accident-prone and mum always used to say that there was a hospital chair with my name on it! Many a time I would go out to play and end up at A & E. We would be out for hours, particularly in the holidays, and only seemed to use home for eating and bed. You could do that in those days without fear or worry. We never strayed too far, just enough to be out of mum's reach.

We would usually be with the Lynches and spend hours hanging around near the railway track, collecting conkers by the bagful near the Princess Parkway and Nell Lane junction and, of course, playing football. If we weren't on Hough End, Peter Ingham and I would sneak into the grounds of Whalley Grange School and use the hockey posts. One place we kept away from was the house just across the road because the man there would put a knife through our ball if it went near. Although Alan was the eldest, he could be a little naive at times and not very street-wise so the lads would often come to me to get things sorted out. I suppose this started the habit of getting things sorted for people as I was to do so countless times on the football pitch, as many an opposition player would testify.

Although mum had a brother who played for Port Vale, she was never really interested in football, or most sports for that matter. I think she was put off because sport was always on television in our house. If it wasn't football or wrestling, it would be snooker, darts or rugby. With all that and the war films, she never had a chance to enjoy programmes that she wanted to watch. She was also well-used to washing dirty football kit belonging to us lot and our mates, and that can't have helped her enjoyment of the game.

I remember mum coming to my debut for City with her sister, Irene, and she came to Tranmere a couple of times, but that was it. That is not to say that she was not proud of everything I achieved in the game and she became something of a celebrity in the area after I had signed for City, always fending off questions about me. She made out that this was a nuisance but, deep down, loved the attention that her kid was getting. I know that she would never let me get too big for my boots, though. She and my brothers have kept me grounded throughout my life. They never let me forget my roots, and this was a massive help to me.

With no dad on the scene and mum having to be at home, I often went to football in my young days envious of others who had their mums and dads with them. They would be there with their flasks of coffee and their deck chairs and I never had anyone, just me and my plastic bag containing Hovis or Sunblest sandwiches. It was a case of 'get your boots on, get out, do your thing and go home again'. I was always the captain, and was expected to lead by example – but in that way I could not. I never resented it because that was the way things were. If mum was to spend hours watching me, others in the family would go without. How I wished my dad could have been able to watch me in those early days – he would have loved it.

One of the dad's did eventually take me under his wing. George Grady's son, also George, was a big mate who I had known for a long time. I used to go round to the Grady's house of a morning before school, and George senior came to watch us, which was good of him.

My mum did everything for us, and only started to get a life for herself as we became more independent. She would go to the local more often with the neighbours. Typical of her, she felt guilty about doing so but it was time for her to have some time to herself and we understood that. She eventually got a job as a carer and really enjoyed it, before she had to be signed off because of her failing eyesight.

As brothers, we were still solidly together as we grew into teenagers. We always wanted to work and we had weekend jobs to earn our own money. There was a seven-year range in age between us. We were close, and still see a lot of each other today. Had we not always been so well-grounded, I could see us going the wrong way. There were other big families of large lads in the area, and some were like gangsters – but not the Nixons. For that we have to be grateful to mum and dad, and to some great mates.

Chapter Four

SKY BLUE DREAMING

'I'd pretend to be them as we played in school... years later, I counted them amongst my friends'

Old Moat Junior School was about half a mile away from Bosley Avenue. It's still there, because I show it to my kids when we are visiting mum. Like places often do when you go back to them, Old Moat looks a lot smaller now and in need of repair. But I am pleased to see that they have just started building a new school which should be completed in 2012.

I would walk to and from school through the estate, turning left and right past familiar houses. On the way home I would often stop off in my den. This was a tiny area by the side of the road, under a lamp-post and covered by a privet hedge. I would sit inside for a few minutes lost in my thoughts and feel like I was king of the castle. The space is still there to this day but without the magic – and without the privet.

My brothers and I were never academic but always sporty – and it was always football. Everyone wanted to be a footballer. During the week, I couldn't wait for Saturday to come round, particularly if City were playing at home. I was told off many a time in lessons at both primary and high schools as my mind wandered in the direction of Maine Road. I would join the thousands of other supporters on the Kippax Stand opposite the main tunnel. The famous home of the Sky Blue fans, named after a nearby street, was unusual among football grounds as it occupied a full side of the ground rather than one end behind a goal.

I could see the ground from my bedroom window. I would walk down past the pig farm with my brothers and Terry Lynch. There would be one or two others as well from time to time. We walked through the back alleys past the bins and the washing hanging out to dry, and see the stadium opening up in front of us. We'd all have our sky blue and white scarves round our necks, and we would always stop for a hot dog whilst we watched all the thousands of excited fans crowding into the ground. I couldn't wait to get inside on to the Kippax to watch the best team in the world. It was just a magical feeling. It did not seem to matter that the electronic scoreboard was slow or that the place needed a lick of paint. The ground was run-down by comparison to the Etihad Stadium today but it was still our special place as we sang the songs at the top of our voices, ready to follow our lads to victory. Maine Road's position within the working-class streets of terraced houses gave it an atmosphere unlike any other.

Then, as the kick-off approached, I would stare across the pitch at my heroes as they lined up ready to come out and receive the cheers from 30,000 fans. The butterflies began to go crazy in the stomach. We would sing the songs, and then watch transfixed as they showed us what they could do well, and how they went about it.

I can remember a League Cup semi-final against Liverpool in 1981, when Kevin Reeves gave us the lead. Everybody threw their ale in the air and it was a beer shampoo all round. Before you knew it, Liverpool had almost scored at the other end and we were back on pins again.

We would watch a great team in action with heroes such as Joe Corrigan, Asa Hartford, Colin Bell and Mike Summerbee. I would pretend to be them as we played our games of football in the school yard and on the fields around the area. Little did I know that, years later, I could count all of those legends amongst my friends.

We would then be glued to 'Match of the Day' on Saturday night if the game was televised. and it would still be the main topic of conversation for most on the Sunday. The whole thing got under our skin and into our blood – it was fabulous. Then, back at school on the Monday, we would practise the shots and copy the moves that we had watched over the weekend.

Old Moat had a school team and I played centre-forward, on a grass pitch which is still there down the side of the school. The likes of Broad Oak and Chorlton Park still come to play, just like they did in my day. I captained the side and was always looked up to as a leader. I had respect and tried to show it – after all, it costs nothing. That is why I sometimes lose my rag at people who do not show respect.

Mr Clare and Mr O'Hara were two teachers who I remember well. Mr O'Hara looked after the sport. He was a well-respected teacher who I owe so much to. I wasn't a big lad at first but one day I woke up and found my pyjamas up to my knees, like Tom Hanks in the film 'Big'. I went for a trial for Manchester Boys in my school position of centre-forward, but

Mr O'Hara decided there were too many centre-forwards all trying to become Frannie Lee so he threw me in goal on a Friday night trial. Without that decision, you might not have been reading this story today.

Things were different in the classroom. I was never going to make the quiz team at school and the only subject that I remember liking was geography. I was fascinated by the different countries on the world map, lots of them coloured in pink as part of the Commonwealth. I am still interested to learn about different countries to this day and am privileged to have visited many through football.

When I went to high school at the age of 11, lots of my mates went with me. There were two choices. You could walk out of our house and turn right to Burnage High, or take a left to Wilbraham High. I turned left and so did three of my brothers, but Philip went to Burnage. We all received benefits which let us buy our uniform from the Co-op. Wilbraham was a new school, about a mile away, and I either went on the bus or walked. One day I was on the bus when I started to get picked on. The lad did not realise it was one of my brothers sitting next to me and he soon got sorted out.

Alan had started at Wilbraham six months after dad died, and that made things easier for us when we arrived. He had been getting bullied by a particular pupil and was convinced one day that he saw an image of dad standing in an alcove at school with his fists up. When the boy started on him again at lunchtime, Alan battered him. He became cock of the school after that and, although he had just about passed through when Leslie, Jason and I pitched up, his reputation remained.

Although we looked after each other, we still missed dad, the father-figure to look over your shoulder for you. Without him, we had to fend for ourselves.

The five Lynches, next door but one, all went to Burnage High, and two others further up the road were always knocking around with us. We all wanted to be each other's mates, and never lost the opportunity to go out and play football. We would always be out on the local pitch, particularly when the nights were getting lighter. We would go to the gym and the swimming baths and everyone would look after each other. After all that exercise we'd come back and eat mum out of house and home.

Through my teenage years I still lived for my sport. If there wasn't a game of football it would be athletics or cricket. Mr Bell was the sports teacher. He used to be a goalkeeper, with Grimsby Town I think. He was a fantastic guy who promoted a great team spirit and knew how to get the best out of you. I seem to remember that he came from County Durham. Mr Bell always wanted to help. He organised and planned everything and we just went out and played.

He also made me captain of the football team. I was still in goal but played upfield as well, although not at the same time. Not even I can do that! I also turned out for the year group above. The side improved, and there were a couple of England youth players. They would go up for their England caps in the end-of-year assemblies and I would think, 'I want a bit of that'. I came across a picture recently showing me receiving some award or other and I was standing in front of the headmaster wearing my scruffy trainers, which had hit a thousand shots in the playground. I didn't even have proper shoes – how embarrassing. I would also go to the school discos in borrowed clothes. Sometimes I had to sew a zip or put a button on myself. I bet John Travolta never had to do that.

Also at Wilbraham was Alex Williams, later to play in goal for Manchester City. Alex was a year above me and neither of us could possibly imagine how things were going to pan out in the coming years. Another future City player at school was Clive Wilson, who was a big mate of Alex's. Clive went through the City youth system and played for the Sky Blues for about eight seasons. He played either midfield or left-back and, after leaving City, went on to more success in London for Chelsea, QPR and Tottenham Hotspur. Clive must have enjoyed school more than I did because he became a PE teacher after he gave up the game.

The Wilbraham teachers that I respected most were those connected with sport, just as they had been at Old Moat. Apart from Mr Bell there was Mrs Addison, who encouraged me to follow my dreams, and Mr Seddon, an ex-rugby player. He was a big growler but, again, had our respect. Rugby was never an option although Bradley, my son, plays and I watch him regularly every Sunday morning. It seems a much more respectable sport in this day and age and the referees don't seem to get anything like as much stick as they do in football. I've grown to like the game so much that last year I took a coaching qualification at Bradley's club. I love to see my lad out in the fresh air and learning rules and manners, as well as having regular exercise. I would have no qualms about him going into football if that's what he wanted, but at the moment he is not built for it.

I left school at 16 with barely a qualification. I virtually walked out, not through being a bad boy but I just could not be bothered. I needed to get out into the big wide world to do my learning – and my brothers felt the same.

Chapter Five

SUNDAY WORST

'On the side of the pitch would be guys with shooters and machetes...'

I didn't hold out any job for that long and worked in most of the shops along Mauldeth Road at one time or another. There was no profession and no apprenticeship because I had no qualifications. I had to get out there and earn some money for my mum and my family. Simple as that.

In 1978 I went to work at B & Q near Old Trafford cricket ground. I stacked shelves and did building and labouring. There was melamine everywhere you looked. At the interview they asked me, 'Do you make tea? Do you drive a fork lift truck?' I said, 'How big's the teapot?' I left after six or seven months. I then worked for James and Bloom, a delivery service which provided parts for shutters on shops. I was also a removal man for Barbers on about £20 a day.

One of my favourite positions was at John Flemings Upholstery in Ancoats. My two older brothers worked there and managed to get me a job as an upholstery cutter. It involved carrying huge rolls of material between floors, dropping them down on to work surfaces 30 foot by 6 foot, drawing templates for things like three-piece suites and cutting them into shape. It was time-consuming but, by the end, I was using equipment which allowed me to put a template on top of 20 sheets and cut straight through them at one go. Health and safety was not as rigid in those days and I got into a few scrapes. One day I cut through an electrical wire and threw myself 12 feet across the floor. I just picked myself up and got on with it. I enjoyed the upholstery job more than most because my brothers were there and there was plenty of banter, mainly at my expense as I was the lone City voice amongst loads of United fans. John Baker, the foreman, was a very nice guy and treated us well. It all made it enjoyable to go to work every day.

When John Flemings closed down I became a car valeter for Auto Cleanse. It was a nationwide company and, originally, I got a position at Ashton through a guy called Terry Gray. He then promoted me to the firm opposite Old Trafford football ground and, without realising, it was to play a large part in this story.

My days started early. A lie-in was not an option for me. I would often get up at about seven o'clock and trot across to Hough End fields, where I would do three or four laps before running to work and back home at the end of the day. A desire to work hard and keep fit was there from the start and it remained throughout my football career. Many a pro regarded me as the hardest trainer they knew. I never eased off, and this all started around Hough End playing fields.

Organised football was beginning to take shape. At the age of 14, I was playing for St Christopher's Church on Saturdays with good friends Ronnie Moreland and the late Billy Lester. St Christopher's was just across Princess Road from Hough End fields and, therefore, not far from my house. I also played for Manchester City Social Club on Sunday mornings. It was next to Maine Road and well-organised. As if that wasn't enough there was Manchester Apollo on Sunday afternoons. Apollo was made up from those of us who used to go down to Hough End playing fields for a kick around. We had nothing else to do then so formed a club which would eventually become one of the most celebrated Sunday League teams over the next decade.

Les would be centre-half and Alan a striker so the Nixon brothers often made up the spine of the teams. Les would achieve success as a semi-pro but Alan would be the first to admit that, despite scoring goals, it was more about being in the right place at the right time for him rather than relying on skill. Apollo had Mark Harrison, who was an older and more experienced keeper than me, so I would often play up front.

The Sunday League was a hard school for a young player, but I enjoyed it so much that I would even turn out after I had signed for City. I'd make sure that I kept away from the thick of the action so as not to get injured. However, when it got around that I was playing I would often get threatened by local gangsters on a Saturday night. They'd tell me what they'd do if I turned out – this, that and the other. That's how it was, then. I had to learn to look after myself pretty quickly because it was the underworld, with gangsters playing football. If you didn't understand the system or look after yourself you'd get hurt.

I remember playing up at Oldham. On the side of the pitch would be guys with shooters and machetes. I've been there, seen it all. I was a young lad surrounded by hardened men who'd done it all non-League-wise. It was tough.

There was a fella called Al Bury. We used to call him 'the Bear'. Al was a fantastic guy and a fantastic player. Leslie and me were playing alongside him once in a five-a-side competition. There were some notorious brothers watching and the next thing we know, these buggers are starting on him and, suddenly, everyone's brawling in the middle of the pitch.

Yes, it was a hard world and when I came into the professional game it meant that I was able to look after myself alongside a lot of other players who had not had that experience. They had been wrapped in cotton wool. After what I'd been through I was not prepared to let others take the piss out of me. That was me then. I was intensely competitive, professional and had bravado. Through learning the hard way, I was able to look after myself and went on to show that on many a football ground from the big stadiums such as Anfield and Goodison Park to countless smaller league grounds dotted around the country.

A guy called Dave 'Taffy' Jones ran a team called Mauldeth, who played against us on Sundays. 'Taffy' was a massive figure around the football fraternity in Manchester and helped lots of players. He was also assistant-manager of Curzon Ashton. The club had a lovely set-up at the National Park near the police station in Ashton, and it was a much better standard. In fact, it was a massive step-up from the level I had been used to at St Christopher's and my other weekend teams.

I went for a trial and had two seasons there before making the first team in August 1982. Jimmy Lomas was their keeper at the time. He was a top player in non-League and I learned a lot from him. As a young lad of 16 I was there to learn. This was a semi-professional level. I looked up to the players around me and took in a huge amount over the next couple of years. When Jimmy missed the match at Prescot Cables because of a heavy cold, I made my debut. The paper said I had 'an unsteady start', but put much of the blame for a 2-0 defeat on my defence. Nothing new there then – I've been blaming defenders throughout my career for going AWOL at the wrong moment! Characters such as Kenny Wolstenholme and Denis Haigh took me under their wing at Curzon, but it was 'Taffy' Jones who was to play a big part in my life and I owe him so much.

After only seven first-team games for Curzon I went for trials at Wigan Athletic, then in the Third Division. The late Harry McNally was the chief scout and while I was there I was to train at Springfield Park, which was the club's home before it moved to what is now the DW Stadium in 1999. I also played for the reserves in a Central League game against Chesterfield.

I would sit in the dressing room at Wigan with the likes of Larry Lloyd, the manager, Archie Gemmell and Paul Jewell. These guys were all professionals as there were no apprenticeships then. There was I with my round of home-made sandwiches quietly taking it all in and looking in awe at these great figures of the game. To give you an idea of how long ago it was, Denis Law was presenting 'Kick Off'. Nothing developed so I went back to Curzon, where I was beginning to get noticed through my performances at non-League level.

Les was playing centre-half for Stalybridge Celtic by now. He was a no-nonsense type of player and we used to have many good battles when Celtic met Curzon in the West Cheshire League. He would come up for all the set pieces but never got any joy, believe me.

He and I had trials for Stockport County who were managed

by ex-City star, Mike Summerbee. We knew that we were paper fillers and that they had people to fill all positions but they might just get the odd one coming through, and we were determined to make our mark. Les being Les proceeded to kick Summerbee left, right and centre and, unsurprisingly, we did not get through. Les was a local legend and once won a poll to name the best non-League player in the area. All his former fans from his time at Droylsden came out and voted for him.

I had suffered a few problems with my back and met a guy on holiday, who noticed that there was something wrong from my posture. As a personal trainer, I now know what it was to do with. He put two thumbs around my lower back muscle and gave me some acupuncture. To this day, touch wood, I have been fine.

The attention I got from the trainer set me up to increase my work load, and I built myself up more and more by increasing the visits to the gym and the running to and from work. I became as strong as an ox and agile.

I was 19 and learning my trade for Curzon Ashton. I was still valeting cars and, as the wash leather went backwards and forwards across the body work, I dreamt of the day when I would become a professional footballer.

Chapter Six

CAN I HAVE A JOB?

'I can't explain how it happened, but on impulse I stopped the car outside the ground'

I was at Quicks for Ford in Manchester, just across from Old Trafford football ground, the 'Theatre of Dreams'. My days were spent sprucing cars up and the work kept me fit and active. One day I was working on a smart 4 x 4 black Sierra Sapphire. I'd just finished after about three hours valeting and it was all 'shiny shiny'. I handed the keys back to my boss, job done. It was about 1pm by now and a few minutes later this big, blond guy comes across the road. My boss gave him the keys to the Sapphire, in he pops and away he goes.

I didn't get a proper look at him but my boss told me that it was none other than Gary Bailey, the Manchester United goalkeeper and, unbeknown to me, we provided him with a car. Gary made nearly 300 appearances for the Reds between 1978 and 1987 and also played twice for England. A posh car would no doubt be one of many luxuries that came with his success and it made me really think about my own position. I had spent many an hour dreaming of being a footballer and I'm sure that some of those cars looked brand spanking new after I had rubbed the bodywork backwards and forwards constantly while I played fantasy games in my head. To play football was what I wanted more than anything. I knew that I had the ability and belief to make it, and I had just seen close-up what a successful career as a goalkeeper could bring.

I finished my shift at about three o'clock and set off home. I never actually planned to stop on the way but the drive back to Bosley Avenue always took me near Maine Road.

I cannot explain how it happened but, on impulse, I stopped the car outside the ground. I suddenly decided that I would go in and ask if they would give me a trial. I took a few deep breaths and got out of the car. I walked towards the main entrance, heart pounding and nerves jangling. I paused after a few steps and thought, 'What if they say no?'

Well, if they did, I would walk back to my car having lost nothing. It was now or never. If you do not ask, you do not get. My mum had taught me that lesson and I pass it on now to my kids and the people I teach. No one else was going to do it for me at that point in my life so I had to do it for myself.

It took a lot of balls, I must say, because the entrance to the ground was impressive. It was like walking into Buckingham Palace. I saw the blue bars down the side of the stadium and went through big metal gates and impressive oak doors. This was certainly not the entrance that I was used to going through on match days. I queued up with Joe Public and squeezed my way through the turnstiles.

Once inside, I walked across the plush carpet and climbed up about 15 steps to a reception area where Julia and Libby, the secretaries, worked. They were strangers then but I now know them well.

Julia looked at me with surprise, clearly not expecting a 6ft 4ins, 15 stone young man in an Auto-Cleanse t-shirt at that time of day. I walked up the stairs, stood in front of them and announced that I wanted a trial for Manchester City.

"I'm a local keeper. Any chance of you watching me?"

After a few moments, during which they did not know quite what to say, Julia replied: "No one asks for a trial like that!"

My response was simple and to the point: "Well, I just have. I'm Eric, I'm a goalkeeper and I'm here."

An internal phone call was made and, before long, three men came out of an office about 20 yards down the corridor. As they walked towards me, it did not take me long to recognise all three of them.

Each was a City legend – Ken Barnes, Tony Book and Denis Law. They were three guys who anyone in the great world of football would wish to meet, and here I was getting the chance on a Friday afternoon as I went home after work. They seemed in the mood for a bit of banter at the end of the week and stood there looking in amazement at the young upstart in front of them. They started asking me questions and here I was, standing inside Manchester City's ground looking at three people who, up to now, I'd only seen on the telly, in my 'Shoot' magazines or on the pitch. I towered over them physically, but their reputations were huge compared to mine.

Tony Book was a former player who made 244 appearances between 1966 and 1974. A full-back signed from Plymouth Argyle, Book was City's most successful captain in terms of trophies lifted. These included the FA Cup (1969), the League Cup and the European Cup-Winners' Cup (both 1970). By the time of our meeting, Book had also been the club's manager.

Denis Law was an iconic Manchester figure. He had a glittering career at home and abroad with his glory days spent at Old Trafford, where he played over 300 games between 1962 and 1973. Law had also played at Maine Road for City, spending two periods at the ground separated by 12 years. He retired in 1974, shortly after his famous back-heel had given City a 1-0 victory at Old Trafford. Law thought that he had condemned his former club to relegation and did not celebrate but, in fact, United would have gone down had the game been drawn anyway. He loved nothing better than to stop by at Maine Road for a chat. I later learned how Denis would be talking ten-to-the dozen and firing out expletives on every second word. If someone he wanted to impress walked into the room he could immediately turn it off and talk respectably without dropping an 'h'. Call it a knack.

Ken Barnes, a fantastic guy who is sadly no longer with us, had played 258 games for City through the 1950s and early '60s. He had returned to the club in 1970 and held a number of different positions within the coaching and management set-up. He met me that day as the chief scout, a role that he was to carry out until 1991. Ken showed the kind of respect that afternoon that I was to see him show me and all players, whether senior or junior, for years after. He said he would arrange for someone to see me play the next day. He was always one to give people an opportunity.

My heart was still beating furiously as I left the ground, taking in the full significance of what I had just done. My family couldn't quite believe it when I told them and I spent a large part of Friday evening thinking about how it might go from here. I was glad I had done the deed, but didn't want to get carried away because nothing had happened yet.

Saturday came. I played for Curzon at Buxton in the FA Cup and we got beat 5-0. I thought that I had been left high and dry by my defenders, and that was the end of my dreams. I was gutted. I would know how to deal with the experience now but back then I was just a kid trying to make an impression and I felt that, after overcoming massive nerves to push myself forward at the ground the day before, I had blown my chance.

I was really down overnight but turned out at centre-forward for my team at Stockport County's training ground on the Sunday afternoon. I scored a hat-trick, which made me feel a bit better. I was about to head off to work on the Monday morning when the phone rang at about 10 o'clock. It was Manchester City, asking if I could play for the reserves that evening against Barnsley at Maine Road.

Could I play? For my home team on the hallowed turf that was Maine Road? It was something that you could never imagine would ever happen in your life, and I could not wait!

I went to work as usual but my mind was racing and I kept looking at the clock. Doesn't time move slowly when you don't want it to? Eventually, I headed home and prepared for my trip to Maine Road.

Barnsley had Mick McCarthy in their side and he would eventually sign for City. We had a team of potential stars of the future including David White, Paul Simpson, Steve Redmond, Andy Hinchcliffe and the Beckfords. They were apprentices who had come through the system of cleaning boots and painting stands, whereas I had served my time in a real harsh world. I was a couple of years older and an elder statesman by comparison, but younger than them in football terms.

I played and tried my best to enjoy the experience as well as learn from it. The final score was 0-0 and I was happy with my performance. My family and friends went, everyone paid their way in to watch me. My first girlfriend, Sharon, was there with her brother, Dean, and they took some photographs. I did the business, got the pictures and then went back to work the next day as if nothing had happened.

City then asked me to train with them so I carried on working for a week or two before committing myself on a day-to-day basis. Mum never really understood what it was all about. My brothers and I carved our own careers and she stayed at home to look after us. I was not on a contract but I was being given an opportunity that millions of others would want. I was getting just £21 a week so wasn't in it for the money! I was determined not to throw away my chance. Training with the first team, I was always part and parcel of what was going on.

I trained through the season and played more games. I was only on expenses but it was worth it to train and play with my heroes. Alex Williams, my old school mate, was the first-team keeper. Alex replaced Joe Corrigan, becoming the first black goalkeeper to appear in the top flight of English football, and made 125 appearances in six years. He was to retire in 1987 due to a recurring back injury. We got on really well, and he taught me a lot. I learned from Corrigan as well and loved watching him. Big Joe made 476 league appearances for City between 1967 and 1982. He had speed, agility and a wonderful attitude. I definitely modelled myself on him and his work ethic still influences the way that I work with goalkeepers today.

A lot of the younger apprentices looked up to me and what I had to offer. I was big, robust and more street-wise. I was the guy who would run to and from work to the gym, carrying 15-and-a-half stone of solid muscle. I never drank, ate the right stuff and lived healthily because I wanted to play for Manchester City. The young lads were a lovely group. I got to know them well and looked out for them, just as I had done with my brothers as we grew up.

Come to think of it, I'm still the same with my brothers now. Even though I'm on the Wirral and three of them live in Manchester near my mum I still tend to get the phone calls to sort things out back home.

The apprentices would always take their fair share of micky-taking from the senior guys, and I must admit I dished a bit out as well when I reached that status. They would have to do anything that was asked of them, and the repercussions for not obeying could be harsh. You could get away with it then and there was no deliberate malice shown. It was just the way of the world, and it often made them better players and people.

I remember just before Christmas stripping one of the young players, putting him in a kit basket and shoving him outside Maine Road for an hour or two because he gave me some lip. The lad was always a bit gobby and fancied himself to be in a boy band. I'd had enough so decided to teach him a lesson. Before he left the building I put him under a cold shower. I was also at pains to warn the rest of the young 'uns that the same would happen to them if they tried to get him out! There was another time when I threw Ian Brightwell through an open window when we went to Sweden on tour because he wouldn't get out of our room!

The club was fortunate to have so many talented young players coming through the ranks, but had nurtured them well and the lads showed their potential by winning the FA Youth Cup in 1986, a sweet victory over United. In the semis they had beaten an Arsenal team including the likes of Paul Merson and Michael Thomas. One or two members of the City side had already been in the first team and Paul Simpson and John Beresford had gone out on loan to Finn Harps in Ireland. All are now household names.

The City squad at the time was far different in make-up to today's multi-national, highly paid group of players. Twelve had come through the club's junior section. Complementing them were signings such as Kevin Bond (from Seattle Sounders), Derek Parlane (Leeds United) and Gordon Dalziel (Rangers).

After three years at Curzon, and as 1983 drew to a close, I had become their third club player in two years to join a Football League club. Winger Steve Wigley was signed by Brian Clough at Nottingham Forest and played over 300 matches for various clubs, while centre-forward Malcolm O'Connor went to Rochdale. I celebrated my last match for the club in style by saving a first-half penalty. Curzon beat Formby 1-0 and picked up £1,000 from City and the promise of a friendly. Chairman Harry Twamley paid me a kind tribute:

"Eric is an ideal build for a goalkeeper and we are delighted at his move to City. He has the ability to reach the top."

I happen to know Gary Bailey now and he's a fantastic guy. Although I did not foresee it at the time, I was to play against him on many occasions and also saw him when I went to study for my UEFA 'A' licence. I got the chance to tell him about the events of that afternoon and he could not believe it. Without realising it, he had inspired me to take the bull by the horns and experience one of those life-changing moments.

Chapter Seven

CITY LIFE

'(Tony) Book gave (Ray) Ranson the scissors. I've never seen a tackle like it in my life'

We trained every morning in our own kit and I even had my own apprentice. I could not believe how fortunate I was. I always arrived early for training, getting to the ground for nine o'clock. I would go various ways over the short distance, then straight down the back of the Kippax and in at the players' entrance past Harry on the door.

First stop would be an hour in the gym. I would be constantly doing sit-ups and weights, and I'm sure some of the other lads avoided coming into the gym when I was in full flow because I'd have a full sets of weights on the equipment. I wouldn't accept second best from anyone at any time and they knew that, so stayed clear. I would devise my own circuits, and maintain flexibility and co-ordination as well as concentrating a lot on strength work. I knew that I wasn't a natural keeper like Joe Hart, but a manufactured one who had started as a centre-forward and that if I was to progress I would have to work twice as hard as the next man. I would go back into the gym after training to do more. My approach was relentless but it was what I felt I needed.

I would take a bag of footballs and my cones and dive around on my own, working on getting my technique right. I always trained hard, and continued to do so throughout my career. Looking back, I'm sure that I pushed myself too hard. There is no doubt that it cost me in injuries towards the end of my playing days. It was all about quantity not quality in those days. No one knew any different then. Today the main messages are centred around diet, health, mental preparation – basically looking after yourself. As a young pro, I just wanted to train 24 hours a day, and no-one ever warned me against doing so. I never looked for a day off, even though people often told me to. My reply would be, 'No, I've worked bloody hard to get this far and I'm not giving it up.' I might have come across as over-enthusiastic, but I don't think you can be too enthusiastic.

I was in the gym on my own one day when a scrawny little fella walked in with a bag of balls. It was Paul Lake, who went on to play for City. We started chatting and I talked to him about the game that players play within the game, if that makes sense. By this, what I mean is you can work all day and night on your physical fitness at home and get no reward at the end of it from the coaching staff at the club, because they don't see you doing it. There are players in the game that do nothing, but make sure they are seen by the coaching staff at the right time. When they turn their back they skip home or out of the gym, but the main thing is that they have been seen by the people that matter...

So I explained this as a senior player to this young lad, who went on to represent his country, how the game works from an early age and although he worked very hard at achieving his goals, a little free advice did him no harm at all. After spending time scrubbing the boots of Alex and myself, as well as some of the outfield guys, Paul played over a hundred games between 1986 and 1996 and achieved England honours at Under-21 and 'B' level before injury cruelly cut his career short. We are still good friends to this day as he is the liaison officer for the former players at the club.

We used to change at Maine Road and then walk the short distance through the terraced streets to Platt Lane. I was alongside the first team straight away, with stars such as Tony Cunningham, Derek Parlane and Neil McNab. I would walk alongside the likes of Mick McCarthy and Kenny Clements, often stopping to have a chat with the neighbours along the way. This really brought home to me how much the club was part and parcel of the community and, sadly, this has now gone with the move to the Etihad Stadium, the new, purpose-built stadium a few miles away to the east of the city.

The pitch we played on is still there, surrounded on two sides by roads and pavements. It has always been like a goldfish bowl and the public would come along to watch or look on as they passed by. As a kid, I was one of those who purposely came along to stare through the railings and watch the stars perform. I would stand behind Joe Corrigan's goal admiring how hard the great man worked and being inspired by him. I would occasionally say something as Joe came close to pick up the ball and he would briefly look me in the eyes. Neither of us would realise at that point that I would one day be on his side of the railings, and that we would become good friends.

Having so many people close by as they trained meant that

players were often prime targets for criticism if things were not going well. You needed a thick skin at times, but it was certainly a good grounding for us. There was plenty of banter among the players, something I was to indulge in constantly throughout my career, but you had to be respectful at the start of the journey. You could not just expect to walk straight in and be yourself. I had to understand the situation. Six months earlier I was paying to watch these players, and now I was training with them.

A big bonus was working alongside former school-mate, Alex Williams. We have always got on, which was very fortunate. It was a privilege to be able to model my game on him and Joe, the best two keepers around at the time, in my opinion. First team and reserves would separate at first. Billy McNeill and Jimmy Frizzell would take the first team while Tony Book and Glyn Pardoe, another City legend, took the reserves.

I had a great respect for Tony Book. Considering that he had been sacked as the club's first-team manager in 1980, he got on with his duties in a dignified way and never rocked the boat. 'Skip' is perhaps the most imitated coach ever. About eight or nine of us would compete with each other to do the best impression of him. I remember an Irish fella called John Clark who did it brilliantly. Whenever you see former players in testimonials it wouldn't be long before they would come out with a Tony Book impression.

A native of Bath, the former bricklayer had a strong southern burr in his voice. His favourite expression was 'for the life of me son'. Book was a good, honest player, who came into the game late. We had some similarities in our backgrounds and there was mutual respect between us. He seemed to like me for the way I had come off the streets and set my stall out when asking for a trial in front of him, Law and Barnes back on that Friday afternoon. Tony Book wouldn't accept second best. He could spot a slacker a mile away and some did not warm to him as a person, or to his methods. As for me, I think he liked the way I tackled training because he often mentioned me to the apprentices. He was authoritarian with an 'iron rod' approach that contrasted with Glyn Pardoe, who was more for the arm around the shoulder.

Book looked after his youngsters and on just my second day at training I saw only too clearly what happened when a harsh tackle came in on one of the lads. A senior player who should have known better did the damage and suddenly you could see Tony Book moving up the pitch to 'give the scissors'. I was to learn that when this happened, someone was for it and the over-eager tackler would be nailed by a tackle from 'Skip' that usually got the message across.

We were playing a practice game on the Maine Road pitch one day, first team against reserves. 'Skip' had filled in at his favourite right-back position because he was still very fit and drifted upfield, identifying Ray Ranson as a target following a foul on one of his lads. Book gave Ray the scissors, and I've never seen a tackle like it to this day. Ranson certainly learned a lesson from that.

Glyn Pardoe was one of those rarities, a one-club player. After becoming City's youngest-ever player in 1962, having not yet seen his 16th birthday, Glyn went on to make over 300 appearances before retiring in 1976 to take up a coaching position within the club. He was a gentle, reassuring influence on the training ground, and a great servant to Manchester City. Glyn was a fantastic fella who earned everyone's respect for the way he was and what he had done in the game. He still loved to take part and displayed his skills in Friday five-a-sides.

Book and Pardoe, those City stalwarts over many games, proved their pedigree as coaches when they guided the youngsters to that FA Youth Cup victory over United. They were two great characters, with a prodigious work ethic that produced many champion players.

Halfway through the sessions we would join together and finish at about 12 noon. After Friday's stint we would go straight to the Blue Room and sign 50 shirts, 50 balls and 50 of whatever else needed doing. This would happen every week. Nowadays, it is hard to get players to sign anything. I can never understand that. For us it was normal.

The training pitch now forms part of the state-of-the-art premises for the Manchester City Academy. The facilities show how much football and my club has moved forward in the 25 years since I was training at Platt Lane. As well as floodlit indoor and outdoor pitches, there is a cardiovascular suite, classes for kids as young as two, boxercise, spinning and even some conference suites! The Maine Road floodlights which used to dominate the skyline and act as inspiration have now, sadly, disappeared, whilst the short journey that I made from the car to ask for a trial with the club would now take me up a cul-de-sac of modern houses.

The whole training experience was an eye-opener, from the hopping on one leg up and down the Kippax Stand during pre-season to the games of head tennis after sessions had finished. We used to get more out of the head tennis than we did the training. Competitive only begins to describe what went on. We would race each other to get a 'match'. The games would take place in an area near the tunnel which was about 20 metres by 15 in size, with an astroturf surface and stone walls. I used to like to challenge the apprentices, and usually battered them! I remember Jim Tolmie being good at it and Roy Bailey, one of the physios. Jim wasn't very aerial but good with his feet. Neil McNab was also good, Kenny Clements wasn't so bad but Mick McCarthy would never play. I was a net man myself and used to terrorise the opponents, particularly the young 'uns. I always used to threaten anyone at the net, 'Don't let your head stray over on this side otherwise you'll be counting your stitches.'

As you got to know them, you quickly discovered that players who you had previously looked-up to were as human as the next person. They swore, and had all the normal mannerisms.

Neil McNab and Kenny Clements were good mates and I struck up friendships with a lot of the lads, such as Kevin Bond, Tony Cunningham, Steve Kinsey and Mark Lillis. I also trained a few times with Tommy Caton, a defender who played 165 games for City and who before the age of 20 became the youngest player in Football League history to reach 100 games at the top level. Sadly, Tommy died of a heart attack just 10 years later. It was a tragic loss – he was a lovely guy.

When we get together these days we talk about the funny things we got up to back then that you could not get away with now. Having eased myself in slowly at the start, I soon gained the confidence to try a bit of Nixon tomfoolery. It's amazing what you remember, and one image I'll never forget is the the sight of Peter Barnes and Neil McNab riding down a road in northern Sweden on a push bike at three o'clock in the morning, but in broad daylight because we were so far north it didn't go dark for months at a time.

There are many tales of footballers squandering their hard-earned on gambling and other vices as they filled the long hours away from training and playing. It never affected me because I never had enough money to stray. Also, I knew that I had to earn my place. I was dedicated to my career, and I was not going to throw the chance away through being reckless. I was focused – but it was at a price. I had to put aside the many distractions that my mates were following. I was usually too knackered anyway, having put everything into training and matches, so a good kip on the couch would be an ideal answer.

Suddenly I was on the team bus and on the team picture. I was in the papers, on TV, in 'Shoot' magazine, signing autographs – amazing. The best thing was having your own kit. Every day I walked around wearing the Manchester City badge. It was an honour and a privilege that I wasn't going to give up easily. I would get to talk with the legends of the game, such as Brian Clough, and as each week went by, I was becoming accepted as part of the club. Every day was a new day and I took nothing for granted.

I was never on the bench for the first team as it didn't happen that way in those days. Alex was the keeper and I kept for the reserves, normally on Tuesday evenings. I played in the Central League at all the massive stadiums – Anfield, Old Trafford, Villa Park. There was no one else so I was likely to get a run of games, although I made sure that no one else would be in the frame. I also played in testimonials, and went to the national five-a-side competition at Wembley Arena. We went down by minibus. Glyn Pardoe was there with us, as was Tony Book and Clive Wilson.

Adjusting from non-League football to playing at the best club in the land was not easy or straightforward and, I'll be honest, it took me two or three years to adapt. I had to be patient and serve my time in order to gather the kind of experience that Alex had gained. That was what I wanted, and I wasn't going to waste a moment or an opportunity.

An important arrival at about that time was goalkeeping coach, Alan Hodgkinson. He just appeared one day and started doing the business with Alex and myself. Alan was one of the first of his kind, an experienced pro who would go to a number of clubs each week specifically to work with goalkeepers. He was a one-club man, having made 675 appearances for Sheffield United between 1954 and 1971, as well as five for England. It was quite a record. He had played at the very top level and had a huge amount of experience to pass on. There's no doubt that Alan played a big part in my development, just as he did with the likes of Andy Goram and Neville Southall.

He moulded me by changing the way I thought about the game and the way I understood it. I was still a raw recruit and his guidance helped take me on to the next level. There's no doubt that he was a fantastic confidante and a 'no-messing' Yorkshire lad. I owe Alan a huge debt of gratitude.

'Skip', Glyn Pardoe, Alan and others were giving me a fantastic grounding and I was learning fast, while my training regime and motivation had made me fitter than at any time in my life. Eventually, I went to see City manager Billy McNeill, and asked where it was all heading. The former Celtic captain had been City's manager since June 1983, his first job south of the border. He secured promotion back to the top-flight after two seasons in charge at Maine Road, and was renowned for a no-nonsense approach.

There had been a couple of matches, against Grimsby and Oldham towards the end of the 1983/84 season, when I had come close to making my first-team debut because of injury worries with Alex. I appreciated the chance that Billy had given me but it was getting towards the summer break, and I decided to make a stand. Billy said he would let me know at the end of the season.

Soon after our conversation, I was selected to play in Stockport County's centenary match. Alex was on England Youth duty for the European Under-21 Championship and McNeill described it as an 'excellent chance to have a really good look at Eric', as well as 'a perfect opportunity for him.' It was the first time that I had played with the first-team players and I had a fantastic game. I remember, in particular, a double save that I made from Oshor Williams. We won 4-0, and in the words of the 'Manchester Evening News':

'Eric Nixon served notice of his challenge when giving an excellent account of himself. Nixon revealed excellent position and handling of the ball. With further outings certain in the build-up for the next term Nixon could be well-prepared to challenge Williams for the first-team spot.'

That performance was enough for Billy McNeill and Jimmy Frizzell to give me a one-year contract. Fellow Scot Frizzell had been manager of near neighbours Oldham Athletic for over 10 years, and had been invited to join City as McNeill's assistant after being unemployed for a while. He was eventually to become manager for a short period following McNeill's departure in October 1986. Despite sharing the same country of birth, that was where the similarities ended as the two guys were quite different personality-wise.

Jimmy was a no-nonsense sort of guy who had an 'old school' approach to coaching. He was quite funny in practice matches because he would stand on the right or left wing and expect me to throw the ball to him at every opportunity. I knew that he would lose the ball nearly every time I gave it to him and make me look like a mug so it got to the stage that, when he shouted, I would throw the ball to the other wing on purpose. Jimmy would then bellow around the ground: "Have ye' got a wooden eye, Nico?"

Finally, I had my own shirt. It wasn't great money or acclaim, but I was playing for Manchester City. I had my own number and identity and I was just happy to be a pro.

It has always been an honour to achieve what I did for City. I know that thousands of kids would have wanted that and here I was, the kid from Hough End playing fields who had walked into Maine Road and asked for a trial. I would now be sharing regular cups of tea with the lovely secretaries who I first met when I introduced myself. Who would have believed it?

I had made a few trips to clubs looking for an opening but knew that I was just making up numbers. Former World Cup winner Nobby Stiles had picked me up outside the Post House when I was 14 and taken me to Preston. I had walked into the dressing room and there were 22 lads. They all knew their positions and they were sorted. I decided from that moment that when the opportunity came I was going to take it with both hands. Now that opportunity had arrived and, as a goalkeeper, there is no better way to take it than with both hands.

I was determined never to forget my roots and, to be fair, my brothers never let me. In the summer of 1984 I watched one of my old teams, Mersey Lights, win the Bobby Charlton Trophy in a local competition. It was a chance to sign autographs and have a kickabout with the youngsters. Following the terms of my signing I went back to Curzon Ashton with a Manchester City team for a pre-season friendly on 22nd August 1984.

Whenever I played in friendlies and testimonials I would treat them like cup finals. If we were up against the likes of Droylsden and Curzon Ashton I just knew that their goalkeeper would think he was better than me. My attitude was, 'I'll show you why I'm standing here and you're standing there. Let's see if you can match it.' I always played out of my skin because I knew that they would be watching me closely, knowing I had come from the very grounds that they played on week in and week out. I had taken the bull by the horns, walked into City, been given a chance to have the life of a professional footballer and worked day and night to improve my game. It wasn't something that I was going to give up easily and there was a pride in the way that I came out to every cross and threw every ball. I left no stone unturned as I showed them why I was a professional, and what they had to do to become one.

I had earned the chance to play for City. I have got the scars to prove it and can watch myself in action on You Tube. I had earned my stripes in the reserves and was privileged to have toured in America, Africa and Australia in pre-season. I had never had the chance to visit these places before, and the best part was that I had no organising to do. Secretary Bernard Halford sorted everything for us.

Everything was a learning experience that would, one day, take me to the Holy Grail. Apprenticeship served, now it was time to step up to the plate and be counted.

Chapter Eight

THE SHIRT IS MINE

'By the way, you're playing tomorrow'

The day that I had constantly dreamt about finally became a reality on 21st September 1985 when I made my first-team debut at home to West Ham United. It was the ninth league game of City's first season back in the top flight. Two wins and four defeats so far had made for a mixed start to the season, and the side was still looking for its first clean sheet.

Alex Williams had been a constant presence in City's goal, but an in-growing toe nail finally ended a run of 112 consecutive senior competitive games and I remember manager Billy McNeill saying to me at the end of training on the Friday: "By the way, you're playing tomorrow." It was quite low-key really and, at first, I couldn't really take in what he was saying. I could not believe that the time had come but you must remember that I had played one-and-a-half to two seasons in the reserves, and was always preparing myself for the day when this was going to happen. Consequently, I was ready to seize the moment. I felt at that point that it was my destiny. I had not come that far and grafted that hard to be denied the opportunity to play for Manchester City's first team, if it was to be for only one game or 100 games. It was really strange that I was replacing Alex in the team, after previously replacing him in the Wilbraham High School team!

Telegrams of congratulations came in. There was one from Curzon Ashton saying, 'Congratulations and best of luck.' Ken Walsh and Manchester Apollo FC sent a similar message, adding: 'Class will always shine through!' The Sunday League secretary, Frank Riding, wrote: 'Success at long last!' Cards came in from friends and family.

That evening I went home and talked to my mum and brothers. I am not afraid to admit that I cried. I thought long and hard about the game, and how proud my dad would have been. I tried to think of it as just another game of football, and it helped me cope with my nerves and apprehension. I hoped that the senior professionals such as Mick McCarthy and Clive Wilson, my old schoolmate, would be on hand to help me. The day could not come quick enough for me.

In the morning I spent quite a bit of my time by myself while the clock turned very slowly. I had to be at the ground by one o'clock and got a lift there. I made sure that I was early and well-prepared, just as I continued to be in my career. I walked through the main doors, just as I had for my trial. I was no longer there as a ball boy and general dogsbody. I was now in the club's first team. I thought of the history, going back over 100 years, of all the great players who had worn the shirt and the fact that all the fans were paying to see me play.

Looking back over my career, I appreciated every game I got for every club but to play for the team you supported as a kid for the first time, and at home, was something very special that does not come to many people. I was determined to savour the moment and desperately wanted to turn that one game into two, then three... I had to make the management want to pick me again by performing well.

I looked at my shirt, with the number 1 stitched on it, my shorts and kit and thought, 'I've done the hard work on the training ground and these are mine today, nobody else's.' I looked through the match programme and saw my picture. Then I went into the gym just next to the tunnel to do a bit of head tennis, have a bit of banter and get a sweat on. That was to become a regular pre-match activity and we sometimes got so carried away with our 'gentle' warm-up that we would be doing it while the Liverpools and Evertons of this world were warming-up outside!

We went out on to the pitch at two o'clock. The crowd was building. The media were there and everyone wanted a story from the debut boy. The microphones were thrust under our noses and eager journalists were all vying for the same words. The camera bulbs flashed – you were just thrust straight into it. You were never taught how to cope. You suddenly had to deal with all the attention without messing up. It was enough to turn a young man's mind but, luckily, I'd watched and listened to others and learned what to say. This was no time to disrespect others keepers. You want more than this game, sure, but at the moment you are just taking the place of Alex Williams for this match.

I remember just standing for a few minutes and taking it all in. I spotted my family. Mum was there, next to my Auntie Irene. Mum's sight was not good so the lads were helping her. Terry Lynch, my very good friend, was also there but, on this important occasion, Sharon was missing. She had booked a Spanish holiday with her friend weeks ago and it wasn't until the last minute that I knew I was in the team. She was disappointed to miss the game as she had waited a long time for this day but it was too late to cancel the holiday.

Sharon Lancashire, my school sweetheart, will always have a special place in my life. She put me on the straight and narrow. We knew each other for about 11 years and would go to each other's houses on the bus. I told her that I would marry her if I played for City, but it didn't happen quite like that! She went on to do a nurse's degree, I got into my football and suddenly space came between us. We could not have kids and the split that eventually followed was mutual. Sharon re-married and adopted two children. I am very happy that things have worked out for her.

The crowd were singing 'There's only one Eric Nixon!' over and over. They knew who I was, the local lad made good, and that it was all happening less than a mile from my home. We warmed up and I remembered shouting across to Mick McCarthy. 'Pass the ball, Mick!' Can you just imagine Mick McCarthy, ex-Celtic, in the same team as me, ex-Hough End playing fields! Mick was to look after me as I was coming through the ranks and I was pleased to see how he went into a successful career in management after he packed in.

There were others around me who I had previously watched live and on TV as a fan. I had trained with them, of course, but this was something else. As I looked around I could see a mixture of youth and experience, of home-grown players and others from afar.

There was Paul Power, another Manchester lad, who had been in the first team for 10 years by then. Versatile in midfield or defence, Paul was to make 445 appearances and score 36 goals in his time at the club. How many times must I have watched him play?

The experienced defender, Kenny Clements, was perhaps the only one who really looked out for me. He told me to relax and that everything would take care of itself. Kenny played 276 league and cup games for City, in two spells between 1971 and 1987. I still know him to this day and we do charity work together. Neither of us was to know that my debut game would be memorable for Kenny as well as for me!

After three successive defeats and no goals, the manager had rung the changes and I was joined in the side by Jim Melrose, who formed a new striking partnership with Mark Lillis. It was Jim's first full game of the campaign as he had damaged an ankle in pre-season at Hull. Melrose had laid the foundation of City's promotion from the Second Division the previous year with six goals in as many games, and the manager was obviously hoping that the Scot could fire his attack again.

Manchester-born Mark Lillis had enjoyed most of his success at Huddersfield, and had come back across the Pennines after seven seasons in Yorkshire. Then there was Sammy McIlroy, the former Manchester United legend, who was in the early weeks of his only season at Maine Road. He had played over 300 games for the Reds and 80 or so for Northern Ireland. He and Mark were later to form a partnership in management at Stockport and Morecambe.

I remembered the game well because I made sure I did, just in case it did not happen again. It was the biggest game of my life and it wasn't going to pass me by. It was time to focus and do my job properly...

On the referee's whistle, we came out into the tunnel. I was surrounded by huge names. Lining up across from me were Tony Cottee, Alvin Martin and Frank McAvennie. I stood immediately behind skipper Mick McCarthy and shoulder to shoulder with Phil Parkes, who played over 300 games in goal for the Hammers. I was standing in the tunnel that I used to look down on excitedly from my place on the Kippax. I made a point of looking ahead to the spot where I had once stood, watched and cheered, allowing myself another reminder of the journey that I had made to the place just behind Mick McCarthy. I used to stand on the Kippax and wonder what was happening in the tunnel beyond where my eye could take me. I imagined myself there one day – and that day had come.

It was an emotional few moments as the teams walked out and I thought to myself that I was here for my family, that I must not waste the opportunity. I looked around at a crowd of 22,000 and took up my position facing the Platt Lane End. The City team lined up for kick-off and read as follows:

Nixon, May, Wilson, Clements, McCarthy, Phillips, Lillis, Power, Melrose, McIlroy, Simpson.

Clements and McCarthy settled me down and gave me some early touches. The rule about passing back was different from today, meaning that I could pick the ball up without fear of being penalised. Cottee shot and I turned the ball around for a corner – my first save. I held the ball comfortably from the corner. Good start!

Unfortunately, West Ham then took the lead. The goal came from McAvennie's persistence in winning the ball from Clive Wilson. The Scottish international made progress down the right before cutting the ball back for Cottee. The prolific goalscorer, now a Sky Sports commentator, would have enthusiastically described his goal in the following way:

'Great work down the right from McAvennie, he squares the ball for Cottee who sends the debut keeper sprawling with a neat side-step before tapping in the opening goal after six minutes! Manchester City 0 West Ham 1!'

Sky Sports, whose ground-breaking coverage was still some six or seven years away, would have returned to the ground for an update soon after as it took us only four minutes to get back on level terms, with Melrose doing the spade work on the right. His cross found Lillis, who turned the ball in off the foot of a post. It was Mark's third goal of the season and City's first since Tottenham defender, Paul Miller, put through his own goal three weeks previously. Despite the joy that I felt, I resisted celebrating openly because in the back of my mind I knew that at some point I would have to make a save to keep us in the game. I have kept that attitude through my football career.

The Hammers remained the more dangerous side, and I had to dive full stretch to turn away an 18-yard shot from Alan Devonshire. City then came back but my debut had an added touch of drama when I collided with Kenny Clements. A ball came over the top into a grey area between Clements and me. Grey is not my shade – things need to be black or white in my mind. I came off my line, punched at the ball and knocked my team-mate out! I had decided to make the ball mine and ended up felling him with a blow to the chin.

Poor old Kenny was taken off for some Epsom Salts and returned several minutes later. The attitude was 'let's get on with it' but I think, in a strange sort of way, that the incident had given me some respect from my team-mates and the fans.

West Ham took the lead five minutes before half-time. West Ham defender Ray Stewart drove a wicked low cross in from the wing and Mick McCarthy stuck out a toe at the near post to divert it past me for an own goal. I'd had little to do in the first half, apart from picking the ball out of the net twice.

We got back to 2-2 early in the second half. David Phillips hit a shot which cannoned off a defender and Melrose pounced to head the ball past Phil Parkes. From that point onward, I did not have much to do. West Ham gave us a couple of scares late on but that was it.

It was a very quick 90 minutes and I thought that I did well in what the Evening News 'Final Pink' described as a 'mistake-riddled match'. City were booed off at the end, but I made sure that I walked off slowly. I would give myself a seven out of 10, although the 'Sunday People' gave me a six! I was erratic at times and blamed myself for the first goal but my handling and kicking were good. My distribution could have been better, but I made saves when I needed to. I did not have much chance with either goal – and Billy McNeill agreed – but, most importantly, I had played for Manchester City!

After the emotional high over the previous few hours and with reporters busily including my name in their match report, it was back down to earth with a bump. Everyone left me and drove home! Each car thought the other was taking me back.

After the greatest day in my football career, I walked home in the rain, in my club suit and holding my precious programme. As I went down the familiar streets, I turned around and looked back one last time at the ground which meant so much to me.

My attachment to Maine Road had always been strong, but after that day in my life it had just got even stronger.

Chapter Nine

'NIXON'S GLORY'

'I experienced a moment which I would describe as the pinnacle of my time at City'

On the Sunday morning I visited the local lads at Manchester City Social Club on Hough End fields. I went down as a fully-fledged Manchester City first-team player, not that I went in gloating or anything. We had a laugh, and I enjoyed the moment. I had started to sign a few more autographs than usual but, otherwise, life seemed the same. I was surrounded by my mates, who were not going to start looking up in awe at me. To them, I was the same Nico that they had grown up with. There was no halo, no pedestal for me to stand on, and that's just how I wanted it to be.

There was certainly a curiosity about me having played and, naturally, the friends and team-mates who hadn't made the pub the night before wanted to know about my first game and hear about the experience. The same happened in the afternoon when I went to see Manchester Apollo, but I did not want it to get the better of me. I was there to see the lads, and I think that I even acted as sponge man!

Three days later I was selected to play against Bury in the League Cup, known at the time as the Milk Cup. The match was played at Old Trafford because police did not think that they could enforce segregation at Gigg Lane, Bury's ground. Bury had a good side at the time including a friend of mine, Lee Dixon. Like me, Lee had gone to Old Moat School and his brother, Gary, was a mate of one of my brother's. Lee, of course, was to go on to great things first with Stoke City then, more famously, with Arsenal and England. He was a great player and a really nice person.

Also in the Bury side was Craig Madden, who scored 129 goals for the club and who I was later to work alongside at Fleetwood Town. We had taken a two-goal lead by half-time but Bury came back in the 58th minute when former Everton player, Trevor Ross, scored a penalty after Mick McCarthy had allegedly handled a shot from Winston White.

In the last minute I experienced a moment which, looking back, I would describe as the pinnacle of my time at City. Bury were awarded a free-kick and Ross was a specialist. He was 30 yards out and struck it magnificently towards the top corner. I came across and moved my feet ready to explode off my quads. I remember thinking as I stretched that I was not going to make it but, somehow, I got a full hand to the ball and turned it against the angle before it cannoned into the Bury supporters at the Stretford End. In many ways, it was the turning point of my City career because, if we were to have drawn 2-2, it might have given some people ammunition to fire at me. Bury manager Martin Dobson told the 'Daily Mail' after the match:

'Their keeper denied us at least a draw. We were all picking the ball out of the net when he appeared from nowhere. But I think we can go to Maine Road and provide a shock.'

Billy McNeill was obviously satisfied with my form, as he told the 'Manchester Evening News':

'I was very pleased with Eric against Bury. The save he made at the end was exceptional.'

Bury did not produce the shock that Dobson was hoping for. We won 2-1 in the second leg, and went through to the next round on aggregate.

I was then selected for the next league game, at Oxford United. We lost 1-0, with the Oxford goal coming from the penalty spot following a decision by the referee which the 'Pink' described as 'harsh'. They nearly got a second, awarded when I brought Andy Thomas down but I got away with that one! With back-to-back wins against West Bromwich Albion and Tottenham Hotspur now a month ago and no other victories to celebrate, we were all under pressure.

Chelsea came next and, for the first time, I was selected despite Alex being fit. The match was at Maine Road and it was a single goal from Kerry Dixon which defeated us. Dixon lobbed the ball over me as I came forward. He said that had I come out fast he would have hit the ball hard, but he sensed that I had hesitated. It was a lesson learned. However, we now had only one point from our last six games – not good.

To make things even worse, in our next league match we were 3-0 down shortly after half-time at Watford. We clawed our way back to 3-2 but it was the failure to hold Watford in the first half which cost us dear.

Another long trip followed, my first visit into London, as we travelled to Loftus Road to face Queens Park Rangers. The club had a plastic pitch at that time, having become the first club in British professional football to install one in 1981. It stayed until 1988 before football legislation banned such playing surfaces. I was to play on all the others at some point, at Luton, Oldham and Preston. They were all different in texture and you had to be very careful as a keeper or you could be caught out quite easily.

We were very much the pioneer goalkeepers in those days and all we learnt about the artificial conditions was what we got from the warm-up before the match. We kept our cards close to our chests and did not talk about how to play on them with other goalkeepers. It was every man for himself!

I will always remember the Loftus Road pitch for the amount of sand that was on it. It was like Blackpool beach. The sand was there to deaden the bounce, but the stuff got everywhere. It was in your eyes, in your gloves, inside your shirt. The ball bounced higher than normal and it took some time to get fully confident about where it was going to land, and how high it would go. Tracksuit bottoms were the order of the day, of course, but I also wore a pair of cricket pads underneath!

The pitches became a bit of a joke, to be honest, and the ball pinged around all over the place. Players slipped and risked getting carpet burns. Fans complained that the football was awful and boring to watch and, one by one, the clubs returned to natural grass.

Despite my reservations about QPR's playing surface, I had a good game. The crucial moment was when I dived low to my right to stop a header from no more than three yards from Leroy Rosenior. The 'Sunday People' ran a heading, 'NIXON'S CITY SAVER', while the 'News of the World' chose 'NIXON'S GLORY'. The 'Sunday Express' wrote about my 'faultless display'. It was City's first clean sheet of the season in the 13th league match.

I think that the manager had thought about bringing Alex back in after the Watford game but he decided to give me another chance at Loftus Road after the midweek game, when we had put six past Leeds in the Full Members Cup. Following the QPR game, McNeill admitted to the 'Star' that:

'Nixon will have to do something wrong to be left out now.'

Meanwhile, a potentially big day was on the horizon. Despite up and down form in the league, we were on course to reach Wembley in the Full Members Cup. The Leeds thumping was followed by victory over another Yorkshire club, with a 2-1 win over Sheffield United at Bramall Lane taking us through to the area semi-finals.

More appearances were to follow. Champions Everton at home in the league, Arsenal at home in the League Cup, Arsenal away in the league – it was a huge step-up from non-League football! Everton boss Howard Kendall was relieved that his side would not be meeting keepers like me every week, adding that my performance in a 1-1 draw had a 'vital impact' on the game. I was making my mark, and enjoying every opportunity along the way.

Playing at Highbury was a brilliant experience. They had marble floors in the changing room with underfloor heating, and I lined up in the tunnel across from the likes of Niall Quinn, Charlie Nicholas and John Lukic. After my displays in the two Arsenal games, the Gunners manager, Don Howe, commented that I had a 'great future'. Paul Power, City's skipper, told the 'Daily Mirror': 'He is so assured for a keeper who has only just come into the side. His confidence is remarkable.'

This was high praise indeed from respected figures in the

game, and I had only played a handful of matches. I was learning fast and doing a decent job. The fans took to me and made me feel comfortable. They used to sing my name, and would have let me know had I not been up to it. I knew all too well how fickle the fans could be having watched the team with them from the terraces for many years. I must admit that I found it difficult to believe that I was living my dream, and kept looking to the spot in the Kippax Stand where I used to watch my heroes. It helped keep my feet firmly on the ground.

During those early days when I was not as much of a household name, I would walk to the ground, just as I had when I was a fan. I did it on purpose to soak up the atmosphere and this happened for the first seven or eight games. I wanted to milk every minute of the experience because I knew that if I did not, it would pass me by in a flash. It is something I preach to up-and-coming players. I would watch the fans as they gathered and enjoy seeing the excitement on the faces of the kids.

I loved to interact with the fans and this continued throughout my career. In those early days at Maine Road there were many regulars who rocked up week-in and week-out. One was Helen the Bell, who used to sit right behind the goal in the front row of the North Stand, sky blue all over and carrying a huge bell which she loved to clang loud and long. Home keepers got used to it, but she sometimes scared the wits out of a visiting goalie. Someone told me that she had a crush on me but, to be fair, I think that she loved to make a fuss of all the keepers at City. She would give us all a sprig of heather and we would, in return, make a fuss of her because she was part of the club and part of what made matchday special. Big Joe would jump over the hoardings and plant a big kiss on her cheek every time before facing up to the top strikers! Sadly, Helen passed away and, with her, went a part of the club's character.

My growing reputation was shown when former World Cup winner, Jack Charlton, selected me in a team of promising young talents to watch out for on television. He went as far as to say that City could have unearthed a keeper to follow in the tradition of Frank Swift and Bert Trautmann. Also in Charlton's 'team' were Martin Keown of Arsenal, Forest's Nigel Clough and Paul Gascoigne, then at Newcastle.

My old school pal, Alex Williams, was graciously praising my achievement but equally determined to fight for his place. Sadly for Alex, a fellow keeper who had helped me so much, he was never to claim his City shirt back. After succeeding the great Joe Corrigan in March 1982, Alex had played every match in two consecutive seasons. In November 1986, he went on loan to Queen of the South before signing for Port Vale, where he ended his career in September 1987 due to a recurring back injury. I learned so much from Alex as well as feeling a special bond with our school background. He was a great keeper and a great guy.

From my debut against West Ham, I played in 34 consecutive league and cup games. I could hardly have believed that would happen back in September. By now I was getting a basic salary on top of which was appearance money – about £150 a match – and bonuses of about £100 a point. I had been let loose in a whole new, exciting world, and soon became aware of the celebrity culture around football. There have always been celebrity fans connected with City. These days there's the likes of the Gallagher brothers and Jason Manford whose dad, Manny, used to go to matches with my brothers and the Lynches. Jason's a mad City supporter and a great lad, who never turns down charity work for me.

As I was breaking into the first team, the likes of Bernard Manning and Eddie Large would come into the dressing room an hour or so before home games and have a laugh with us, as well as getting a few things signed each time. They would then retire to Roy Bailey's physio room while we had our final team talk from the manager. In return, we would visit Bernard's Embassy Club in Manchester and watch Little and Large, two of our greatest fans, doing shows in Blackpool.

Personalities like that were in awe of you as a player. You were their idols, playing for their favourite team and getting a chance that they never had. The celebrity and the footballer understood and respected each other, and then met somewhere in the middle for a laugh or two and a few drinks.

To add to all the excitement, towards the end of this first full season in the first team I was to experience a weekend when, on successive days, I played in the ultimate derby match and a Wembley cup final!

Chapter Ten

PERFECT WEEKEND

'The sound of 30,000 fans singing "There's only one Eric Nixon" will live with me forever'

I still tell my children about it today, about the time that I first played at Wembley. Not every parent can do that, and it makes me feel privileged. City eventually reached the final of the Full Members Cup and were to play Chelsea on Sunday 23rd March 1986.

The Full Members Cup was a competition which came out of the ban on English clubs in Europe following the Heysel disaster. Ours was the first final, and the competition lasted until 1992 and was also known from time to time as the Simod Cup and the Zenith Data Systems Cup. Although it was not the FA Cup and it received a lot of criticism, it was still a big deal for a young professional aged 23 and fans who had not seen their side lift a trophy for 10 years. The competition was open to First and Second Division clubs, and 21 teams had entered that season. The sides involved were full members of the Football League with full voting rights – thus where the name for the competition came from.

It shows how times have changed in the last 25 years because on the day before the Wembley trip we had to play Manchester United at Old Trafford in the league! I cannot see that happening today. We had already lost 3-0 to United at home, seven days before I made my first-team debut. Now I was going to make the short distance across town to play the team that most of my family, including my late and much-loved dad, had supported all their lives. You can imagine the atmosphere around the house and in the neighbourhood leading up to the game. It was my 26th league match, and the highlights were to be screened that night on 'Match of the Day'.

We got on the team coach at Maine Road and as we slowly approached Old Trafford the driver negotiated carefully through the masses of fans before the police guided us into the tunnel under the stand. Ron Atkinson was the United manager at the time and the Reds team was stacked full of football legends such as Gordon Strachan, Mark Hughes, Frank Stapleton and Norman Whiteside.

As we emerged from the tunnel we turned to the right and ran towards our own fans. There was a sea of sky blue facing us with a mass of red at the Stretford End. The attendance was 51,274 and the occasion made the hairs on the back of your neck stand up. I have already mentioned the other great games I had been involved in during my first season, but this took it to a whole new level.

We matched United toe for toe but went behind when a Colin Gibson free-kick at the Stretford End got through the wall and defeated me to my left, which was disappointing. United had further chances but I was making saves and my distribution was good so the confidence was rising. In the second half, Hughes cut in from the left and had his legs taken away from him by Nicky Reid. Looking back on YouTube, I am amused to see the dramatic protests coming from Neil McNab and others because it looked a nailed-on penalty to me. I went to my right – wrong choice. Strachan shot to my left. We duly went two goals down and you can just imagine the atmosphere as the Reds supporters taunted the Sky Blues at the opposite end of the stadium.

We struck struck back though. Paul Simpson crossed from the right and a United defender deflected it into the path of Clive Wilson, who stooped low to head the ball past Chris Turner. A second goal followed, a bizarre one, when Arthur Albiston swung at the ball on the edge of the area and struck it past Turner. Everyone was going mad! It was a firecracker of an atmosphere, absolutely mental!

I remember going down and taking the ball cleanly at Peter Davenport's feet as he cut across the area from the left. I also made a similar save to deny Strachan after he had linked with Hughes. Close to the end, Hughes got in front of Mick McCarthy and headed just over the bar. I left it nonchalantly, but it was a close shave for us. We eventually took the point and left the ground in good spirits. I was happy with what I had done to help get the draw.

There was little time to reflect as we had to quickly turn our attentions to the Full Members Cup final in less than 24 hours. Not getting beaten at Old Trafford was a boost to our confidence, but we could not celebrate as we boarded the coach and headed straight down to London.

We had one or two injuries that needed some physiotherapy before the final but, thankfully, I was fine and raring to make the most of the occasion! A previous trip down there for the five-a-side tournament was like nothing to this and, fortunately, Wembley trips were to become regular occasions throughout my career. It was a big day for the club and I remember all the youth team being taken down to support us, along with our thousands of devoted fans

Coach journeys then were different from today, mainly because players did not have the various i-pads, phones and mini-computers that occupy them now. I usually sat next to Neil McNab and Kenny Clements. I was still a little restrained on the journeys, taking care to ensure that I was accepted by the group. That can take time and I more than made up for my reserved approach later in my career!

We sat at our London base and watched a video of our opponents, as well as getting an assessment of the United game from the management. I was in bed by 10pm, followed by a good breakfast the next morning. The morning passed slowly but, eventually, the time had come. We were suited and booted and on the team coach heading for the ground.

It was a magical experience winding down Wembley Way, and I remember both sets of fans cheering their teams, with the police cars and motorbikes guiding our way, lights flashing. I can see the coach backing into position and the dressing room with the butler standing in one corner, wearing white gloves and serving tea or coffee! It was huge. The communal team bath was huge – everything was huge!

We looked through the match programme, a familiar ritual for players at all levels before matches. We wanted to know what had been written about us, and whether the picture was complimentary. Then it was the time to have a look at the pitch and surroundings inside the stadium. I remember the canopy of the tunnel and two massive scoreboards. I remember seeing programme sellers beginning to take up their positions. Nerves were beginning to take effect as we walked round, with about two hours still to go before kick-off. There would be over 67,000 spectators making their way to the ground as we took stock of the situation.

I had a few moments to myself. Walking into the furthest goal from the tunnel, which was at the end of the stadium in those days, I turned around and looked down the length of the mighty stadium in front of me. Here I was, the lad from Withington, getting ready to play for a top-flight club in a cup final at the country's international home! It doesn't get better than that. Fairytales do come true after all. I thought how I was doing this for my family and friends. Many of them were going to be there to watch me and my brothers had organised the distribution of tickets. There wasn't a young footballer anywhere who would not have wanted to be where I was at that moment, and I felt very honoured. I had saved a penalty in the Northern final against Hull City so nobody could question my right to be there.

My few moments of thought and reflection were massive for me. I thought about my dad and how proud he would have been. What a weekend he would have had. Firstly, seeing me playing against his beloved United, and then making the journey south to cheer on Eric Junior at Wembley. He wouldn't have had a voice left by Sunday night!

It was a sunny day and we found time for a bit of banter to ease the nerves as we left the pitch. The manager read out the team and we started our preparation. I put on my grey goalkeeping shirt with black trims and the special commemorative badge. I still have it to this day. As we got ready, we could hear the crowd getting louder around the stadium.

A quarter of a century later, I can still remember the sound that my studs made on the hard ground as I walked back up the tunnel for the warm-up, bouncing a ball. The City fans were right ahead of us and I was one of the first players out into the open. The euphoria experienced at moments like that never diminishes with time, and I still get goose bumps when I think back. The sound of 30,000 City fans screaming 'There's only one Eric Nixon!' will live with me forever. If I was able to stop time at any moment it would be then.

Strangely, it was possible to pick out familiar faces in the huge crowd because you knew where they would be in the stadium beforehand. I acknowledged my family and friends with a wave but then it was down to business, and I wanted to make my impact on the game.

Warm-up over, we walked back to the changing rooms for the last few crucial minutes before kick-off, and then lined up in the tunnel. It has never ceased to amaze me how many top quality players I have rubbed shoulders with in the moments before a game and, on this occasion, I looked across to see the likes of David Speedie, Nigel Spackman and Pat Nevin. Pat and I would walk out together as team-mates on many occasions in the years to come.

There was also defender Doug Rougvie, who I was to meet in a bar in Dubai a couple of years ago. It was great to see him and have a good natter about the match. The Chelsea goalkeeper was Steve Francis, who spent much of his time at Stamford Bridge as number two to Eddie Niedzwiecki. It's interesting how both teams, unlike today, were completely made up of British-born players.

Chelsea were the favourites, flying high after spending a 'few bob', whereas we were in a period of transition. After getting promotion, our season had been inconsistent. Our mixed start was followed by five consecutive wins through January, but we had not won since.

The teams were presented to notable actor and director Richard Attenborough, before a match which absolutely flew past. I have to watch the highlights, along with Tony Gubba's commentary, on YouTube these days to remember what actually happened. Looking back, I felt that I could have contributed more to the game had I known then what I know now with the benefit of experience.

The footage shows that Chelsea led 5-1 at one stage, largely thanks to a David Speedie hat-trick, which was the first in 20 years scored at Wembley. However, we scored three times in the last five minutes and gave them a massive scare. We were heading for a real thrashing before the comeback.

My brother, Alan, and his mates obviously thought that as well and had left the ground and headed off back to the coach before the late flurry of goals went in. Chelsea were certainly relieved when the final whistle went. They played in an unfamiliar all-white strip, and the six-minute segment of highlights is action-packed. Substitute Paul Simpson's wing wizardry played a big part. Mark Lillis scored twice for us, including a late penalty, Steve Kinsey got on the scoresheet and there was an own goal by Rougvie.

In the end there was a mixture of defensive lapses and my own lack of experience had cost us but, in the words of the City-loving Gallaghers, those great Manchester musical brothers, 'Don't Look Back in Anger'! A couple of years ago, a panel of experts in the 'Daily Mail' placed the match 38th in a top 50 poll of all the finals played at Wembley in all the different competitions played at the stadium over the years.

The occasion seemed to get to us. We followed Chelsea up the long flight of steps and I remember thinking how much the crowd was in your face and close-up.

It struck me as being a potential security issue, and I still think of it that way when I see the teams going up the steps today. After the match, I mingled in the hospitality suites upstairs, and shook Attenborough's hand once again. To quote one of his best-known films, we had almost made our own 'Great Escape', having come back from so far behind!

Soon we were travelling out of town back up the M6. That night I headed to the local with Terry, Shaun and others, and I looked back with my mates on a memorable weekend that had shown how far I had come as a professional footballer.

Chapter Eleven

FOUR DIVISIONS IN ONE SEASON

'When the Loan Ranger returned, Jimmy Frizzell had to introduce me to the players'

We had Monday off, but were back in training on Tuesday and I returned the better for my experience. I felt that I was growing in stature and also becoming a more obvious part of the scene around the club. I remember talking to Joe Corrigan about the Wembley experience, and how I might learn from it and benefit the next time.

I played in the next league match, at home to Aston Villa. We drew 2-2, but two days later my rising confidence was dealt a major blow. I was left out of the side at Anfield an hour before the game, making way for Barry Siddall, who had come on loan from Stoke City. It was Billy McNeill's way of keeping my feet on the ground, and it was an example of tactical management which I firmly disagreed with at the time – and I still do today. Siddall kept his place for the next five games before I returned for the final game, at home to Luton Town, to end a season which had been memorable for me personally but, for the team, less so. Having been promoted a year ago, a final position of 15th and a points total of 45 was a disappointment for the dedicated City fans.

Despite being pleased with my performances during my debut season, news soon came through that City were about to sign England Under-21 international Perry Suckling from Coventry City. I felt hard done by and Suckling duly started the 1986/87 as first choice. This was to be expected as money had been spent to get him but there was no way that he was a better keeper than I was. Perry was a cocky, chirpy Cockney-type, and quite different in personality from me.

Those around me were very supportive. People were telling me that I was a good keeper but, in my mind, politics was keeping me out. You ask any City fan today and they would say that I should have been in the team in August 1986. As it was, I did not appear in the league again until April 20th!

So began an unusual and record-breaking few months during which I became the first player in the history of the game to play in all four divisions in the same season! I'm sure it must have become a question in a thousand and more pub quiz nights since. It happened as a series of loan arrangements were set up to allow me to get first-team football. City had a reserve keeper in Steve Crompton and he would gain useful experience at the same time. It was a wrench because I still held hopes of carving out a long career at Maine Road but, nevertheless, I felt then that it was the best way forward.

First up were Wolverhampton Wanderers. Sammy Chapman had resigned at around the start of the season, and former

Aston Villa striker Brian Little had been appointed caretaker prior to Graham Turner taking over. Turner kept me on so I must have been doing something right. I went to Molineux for about three months, making 16 appearances. With the club being in the Fourth Division, I had not had much previous involvement with them. It was their first experience of that level and debts had mounted. Wolves were in dire straights and going nowhere. You had to scramble for training kit and then you would find that there were only about six practice balls to kick around – and some of those were ropey! I think the club had to borrow a training ground from a local school. I stayed in the Midlands with Jack and Olive, two club stalwarts who really looked after me. My brother, Alan, was pleased at the time because he was fond of Wolves, inspired by the likes of Derek Dougan. Despite the problems off the pitch, I enjoyed playing for them. The fans remained loyal to their team and as the loan period ended it became clear that Wolves wanted to buy me but I stood my ground and went back to City.

Amongst the squad was a raw, unassuming lad named Steve Bull. I went on to have some great battles with Bully, who became the club's leading scorer with 306 goals, including 18 hat-tricks – what a player he was. Andy Thompson came to Wolves at the same time as Bully, and was another favourite with the Molineux faithful. Many years later we were to link-up again in the Masters. My last game for the gold and blacks was a 3-0 home defeat by Wrexham, and coincided with the first sighting at Molineux of both Bull and Thompson. I was to see plenty of both of them in the coming years at Tranmere v Wolves matches and even more of 'Thommo', who came up to Tranmere for two or three years towards the end of his playing career. I also knocked around a lot with another Wolves legend, Andy Mutch, who was a great lad known for his striking partnership with Bull.

Amongst other things, the experience had left me with eight stitches and a permanent scar above one eye courtesy of an over-physical Rochdale player!

Almost immediately I was back on the road again. This time it was east along the M62 to Bradford City in the Second Division. It was a brief and not very happy part of my career. After achieving so much in my first season at Maine Road, I suddenly felt that I'd come off the rails. Confidence is a massive thing for a goalkeeper because you're out there in the firing line and often isolated – and mine had suddenly dipped. I had the Bradford fans, rightly, on my back as I put in some of the worst performances of my career. This was in no way a reflection on the club itself and the manager, Trevor Cherry, was brilliant. It just did not work out for me, and it was a massive learning curve. Fortunately, I was able to put that right further down the line when I was to return to the Yorkshire club for a second spell.

December 1986 saw me heading south. Chris Nicholl, the Southampton manager, took me on as their England goalkeeper Peter Shilton had a broken nose. I went down on my own and it was Christmas time. All the hotels were closed and I was put in a B & B. I had tomato soup on Christmas Day! It was the furthest I've lived from home. I made my debut against Manchester United at The Dell alongside the likes of Jimmy Case and Mark Wright. We drew 1-1, and followed it up with a 2-2 draw against Chelsea. I also played against Oxford United, including John Aldridge, and Arsenal. My fortunes suddenly rose again, and I was pleased with my form. A move would have been nice but the Saints also had Tim Flowers on their books. I was a stop-gap but did myself a lot of favours by going down to the south coast. I loved every minute and learned a huge amount from Shilton, the ultimate professional, who helped my confidence, had a fantastic attitude towards training and really explained the importance of footwork.

Back at Maine Road, Billy McNeill had been replaced by assistant Jimmy Frizzell. City had only won five league games before Christmas and they were struggling. Despite the Bradford experience, I came back with rave reviews in the papers, on television and radio. I had done the rounds and thought that I would get another crack in the first team.

It was at that point that Harry Gregg, the former Manchester United goalkeeper, approached the club. He asked if I could join him on loan at Carlisle United, then in the Third Division. I still did not seem to be getting anywhere at City, and felt that Gregg's experience would be invaluable. His training methods were often unconventional. He made us take our gloves off in snow and rain, he'd smash the ball at our faces and if we missed the ball it was down to us. That was his way – and it sure made you catch the ball! I enjoyed life at Brunton Park, rooming with Scott McGarvey and Garry Worrall, both ex-Manchester United players. I played well in front of some pitifully small crowds and completed my tour of the divisions! All this achieved in less than 40 matches!

I was never really sure whether it was a good or bad way to enter the record books. Despite it being so unusual, the only guy to mention the achievement was Peter Gardner of the 'Manchester Evening News'. It seemed at the time like the kind of record that would never be equalled but it was. My 'feat' was repeated some 15 years later as Tony Cottee completed his set when on debut for Millwall. It was to be the last season for the ace goalscorer who had put the first goal past me in a league match, and his travels had taken him from Leicester City (Premier League) to Norwich City (First Division), Barnet (Third Division) and on to Second Division promotion-chasers Millwall on deadline day. Like me, he wasn't sure whether it was a good or a bad achievement to be linked with.

I always got on very well with the lads at each club I went to but it was still easy to feel like an outsider. Whenever the 'Loan Ranger' returned to City, Jimmy Frizzell had to 'introduce me' to the players! Things got to the stage where I would be back in Manchester on the Monday morning and by the afternoon two or three clubs would have rung up to see if I fancied having another loan period.

It was an unusual experience, but one that had taught me a lot. Although I found the standard of goalkeeping to be very high across the divisions, my experience certainly taught me never to become complacent and brought home how lucky I was to be at a leading club. I definitely came back a better keeper and more mature as a person. I'd had an experience that no other keeper could ever hope to match, and been given the kick up the backside that I needed. I'd achieved top-flight football within two years of playing non-League, and it had gone to my head. I had stopped putting in the work required to justify my standing. I needed to improve my attitude and I resolved to battle for my place, continue to put everything into training and demonstrate once and for all that I was ready.

I finally put my City shirt back on as the season drew to a close. The game was at Hillsborough on 20th April. We lost 2-1, but I kept my place. Despite two wins and a draw in the last four games, we were relegated. I got some stick, but had only played five times!

Chapter Twelve

MOVING ON

'I had been given the nickname 'Cinderella' – always late for the ball!'

The 1980s won't be remembered with a lot of affection around the blue part of the city, having lived through a series of promotions and relegations and nine managers. City didn't, of course, have the money then that they have today. I don't think that they started to recover strongly until Peter Reid became manager in 1990, when the side finished fifth in the top flight on two successive occasions.

The 1987/88 season began with a home fixture against Plymouth Argyle, and I kept the jersey. Prior to that, some morale had returned to the club when we finished third in an international tournament held at Maine Road. Despite losing to Manchester United, the eventual winners, we bounced back to beat Dutch champions PSV Eindhoven 3-1. Both Paul Stewart and Imre Varadi had been knocking them in for fun in pre-season, with 17 goals between them on the successful five-match Scandinavian tour. They were the match-winners against PSV, with Stewart scoring twice and Varadi once. The City side contained six former youth-team players.

Mel Machin had replaced Jimmy Frizzell as manager. Mel came from Norwich City and there was an early opportunity for him to get to know all the players as we had a tour to West Africa on the go! However, I didn't get on well with Mel as he had his favourites, and I never felt as if I was one of them.

I really wanted to establish myself as the manager's first choice, but had a nervous game against United in the pre-season tournament. Looking back, it was probably one of my worst performances for City. However, my display against the Dutch was described by the 'Manchester Evening News' as 'composed and confident'. The article noted, in particular, a 'superb flying save' four minutes from time.

I had done enough to get the nod from the manager and took my position as number one goalkeeper for the first time at the beginning of a new season. Machin kept faith with a young side for the visit of Plymouth, in keeping with his team selections through the friendlies. City's young guns tore into Argyle from the kick-off, delighting a crowd of around 20,000. After a long trip north the visitors were getting a battering and it was a real surprise, therefore, when Plymouth took the lead through a Nicky Law header in the 35th minute. However, second-half goals in the last 10 minutes from in-form Stewart and Varadi gave us a winning start to the new campaign.

Despite the result, I was angry as I left the pitch. A certain section of the City fans had made it very clear that they did not want me in the side. Once the Plymouth goal had gone in, they started chanting Perry Suckling's name. It is part and parcel of the game and it upset me, but I was determined not to let it affect my performance. I felt cheesed off that they had got on my back after just the first goal of the season – and a superb header at that. I now had three challenges ahead of me. In addition to helping City regain their place in the First Division and remaining as number one goalkeeper, I now had to win the fans over as well.

I kept my place as we made the short trip to Oldham a week later. There was already a lot of talk over my position in the side after the nervy start against Plymouth. Twenty-four hours earlier, Machin had given Perry Suckling a vote of confidence, and many of the column inches in the Sunday papers the next day focused on my position in the side. The 'Sunday Mirror' talked about the pressure surrounding me, but also described in detail a 'world-class save' that I had made at Boundary Park on the stroke of half-time. Andy Ritchie sent a header on target but I was able to twist acrobatically and parry the effort. As Ritchie pounced to finish the job I made a second stop. The striker later admitted that he did not know how I possibly got to the ball. Tommy Docherty, the former United manager, watched on from the stand and ranked the save as good as that made by Gordon Banks from Pele in the 1970 World Cup.

Afterwards, Machin acknowledged that the save kept us in the game, but suggested that my positioning was not as it should have been. We drew 1-1, after taking an early lead through Varadi, and I was happy with a number of important saves. I was perhaps at fault with the Latics equaliser but the 'News of the World' credited me with playing an important part in gaining the point.

I had perhaps become a touch complacent and was determined that it would never happen again. In fact, I came in for extra training on my day off following the game at Boundary Park. In an interview with 'Metro News', I added:

'I've taken some stick from the fans but they pay their money and have every right. Joe Corrigan took a lot more than me and became one of the three best goalkeepers in the country so if I can do as well as him I'll be more than happy.'

It was not the best start to the new season, but I was the man in possession and I was determined to keep it that way. I was finding it hard to win over the fans and, to be fair, so was Perry. They did not seem to remember that I came to the club from just down the road in non-League and only cost the club £1,000. Not a bad bit of business when you think about how much the modern City stars have to do to earn a grand! Perry was in his early 20s and did not cost too much either.

I kept thinking of my family and what they had done for me. They were never far from me on the pitch because I always placed a bag in the corner of the net at the start of each game and, alongside the cap and gloves, were a good luck charm along with photographs of my wife and parents. There was no way that I wanted to be back on the road again like the previous season, other than on the City first-team bus.

Three days after the match against Oldham, Perry was injured at Bloomfield Road. It was during a Central League match and he was accidentally kicked in the face by Blackpool striker Simon Rooney. The injury required 15 stitches in deep cuts around his eyes.

I remained in the first team, heading down the M6 to Villa Park. Aston Villa had finished bottom of the First Division in 1986/87, one place below City, and, despite this, were hailed as promotion favourites. However, it seemed that we had survived the trauma of relegation better than the Midlands giants.

With five teenagers in the side, we came back from being a goal down to earn a draw following Ian Scott's first career goal. We maintained our unbeaten start to the season although the defence was a worry, particularly from set pieces, but my shot -stopping ability was receiving encouraging comments.

The next match, at home to Blackburn Rovers, added fuel to the fire. Not only did we lose for the first time, but I failed to deal with a cross from a free-kick on the left late on from which Rovers scored the winner in a 2-1 victory. The crowd were on my back immediately and booed each touch. They did not give up until I had disappeared down the tunnel at the end of the game. The papers were full of speculation surrounding Perry Suckling's potential return to the side and I had been given the nickname 'Cinderella' – always late for the ball! It seemed that every mistake was being jumped on, and that did not help my confidence.

At about this time, the 'Manchester Evening News' carried an article in which Joe Corrigan spoke passionately about the need for clubs to consider appointing goalkeeping coaches. Joe claimed that if he had had the help of a figure such as Bert Trautmann, the legendary City keeper, he would have made the grade quicker. Alan Hodgkinson, you will remember, had been a big help to me but he was sharing his expertise around a number of clubs so he could not offer daily input. Nowadays, the position of goalkeeping coach is common-place in clubs across the land. Even non-League clubs have them and, indeed, I was to become a goalkeeping coach myself.

I kept my place for the trip to Gay Meadow to face Shrewsbury Town and it was to be the first clean sheet of the season, a goalless draw. A huge army of City fans had travelled down and I had a good game, with one particular save just after the break from a David Linighan header attracting favourable comments in the press coverage. Peter Gardner in the 'Pink' described it as 'breathtaking'. After the match, Mel Machin praised my work ethic, talking about how I apply myself every day and how I 'show the right attitude towards the job.'

I went on to keep two further clean sheets within a week of the Shrewsbury game. Both matches were at Maine Road, where we beat Millwall 4-0 and Stoke City 3-0.

Three days after the Stoke game, on 22nd September, City entertained Wolverhampton Wanderers in the first leg of the League Cup second round. We lost 2-1, and the error that gave Wolves a late victory cost me my place. The manager was furious with the side and with me, particularly with the way in which I had conceded Robbie Dennison's goal from distance.

Perry Suckling had been ruled out for six to eight weeks following a cartridge operation. This latest setback occurred when he injured his knee in training, and then aggravated the problem in a Central League match at Liverpool. With young Darren Williams the only other keeper on the books, Mel Machin was forced to make hurried arrangements to bring in Bobby Mimms from Everton. There was a suggestion that this could lead to a possible permanent transfer at the end of the month's loan period but, at the time, Machin was keen to tell the press that I would be able to learn a lot from an experienced keeper like Bobby. By that stage he had played around 100 games for Rotherham United and Everton, and went on to play over 300 more times for a variety of clubs including Tottenham Hotspur and Blackburn Rovers.

Mimms played in the next three league matches and, three days after, we were due to travel to Molineux for the return leg of the Littlewoods Cup. Everton did not want Mimms to play as he would be cup-tied so it meant a return for me. City's away form was poor, but we won the game 2-0 thanks to goals from full-backs John Gidman and Andy Hinchcliffe, while I went from zero to hero. After all the flak that I had received, I was relieved to get the game under my belt. It was the first away win since January 1986, some 21 months ago, and my mate Neil McNab and I were the only survivors of that victory at White Hart Lane.

Mel Machin sprung to my defence, telling the 'Daily Star':

'He's taken a lot of stick and I've given him plenty but I've always stood by him because I know what he is capable of.'

The 'Daily Express' described my display as 'faultless', but I seemed to be attracting all manner of opinions in the national and local press. A lady from Royton wrote to the 'Pink', urging people to give me a break:

'People have short memories. It was two years ago that Nixon saved a penalty in the Full Members Cup which enabled the team to get to Wembley. He was dropped the following season and went out on loan, but came back more experienced. People should look at the team as a whole and stop pointing the finger at the goalkeeper.'

I was hoping that the reprieve and the good performance against Wolves would lead to a period of stability, not least because my wife Sharon and I had just moved into a new house. My wish was helped by the news that Everton were recalling Bobby Mimms ahead of time as their regular keeper, Neville Southall, had an injury.

A return to league action followed, against Sheffield United at home on the Saturday following the Wolves game, 10th October, and I was back into the headlines. The knives appeared to be drawn again as I was blamed for gifting United a late winner. I palmed away a cross from Colin Morris and Tony Philliskirk headed home. Philliskirk, to be fair, backed me and pointed more to the quality of the cross from Morris. There was no criticism from the dressing room either but it seemed at this stage of my career that it did not take much to get sections of the City fans on my back. It was a case of one step forward and two steps back.

It was very hurtful and an experience that I have never forgotten about. You constantly felt that you were on the edge. There were times when I sat down and thought whether it was worth the hassle. Would I be better off back with my mates enjoying local league matches every weekend? I had to grow up fast and would not want anyone else to go through what I did. I have deliberately kept the critical press cuttings as well as the positive because I think that you can turn such a situation into a positive. It is all about dusting yourself down and facing life. They were undoubtedly uncertain times, and the only way you knew you were getting a new deal was if there was a new pair of boots at the end of the season! However, I got back into work each day determined to do my best because you never know what is round the corner, and that is what I tell young players today. It was a character-building exercise for me.

I will always be grateful to Billy McNeill for giving me my chance. He is undoubtedly a legend in the game but, to be honest, we did not get on and, at the time, I did not like the bullying tactics that he used. However, I didn't understand how the game was played and how professional it was. I failed to appreciate back then that he was bullying me for a purpose, and that was to get me into his first team. It didn't rest easy with me as a raw recruit but, looking back, I now appreciate him in a way that I didn't at the time.

You have to remember that Billy was one of the first British champion footballers. I am full of admiration for what he has achieved in the game. He was then what I am now, a seasoned professional who had been there and seen it all. I was one of his first English signings. Until then he'd gone for fellow Scots such as Derek Parlane, Jim Tolmie and Neil McNab.

Derek had been a Rangers legend through the seventies, racking up 300 games north of the border. There's not so much heard about Jim these days. He was only pint-sized but was a heck of a player who scored about once every four games for City. As for my mate, Neil, he had come to Maine Road via Spurs, Bolton and Brighton and was at the heart of the team through most of the eighties, with over 220 starts.

Although he was not a goalkeeping coach, Billy McNeill did give me one brilliantly simple piece of advice in training:

'Eric, don't wait for the ball. Go and attack it.'

I still use that philosophy today. It is so basic and I took it with me everywhere I went over the rest of my career.

Mel Machin did not give me the rub of the green. To me, he was a big-time Charlie who had not achieved any great shakes as a player or as a manager, but was quite content to try and ruin my career with my beloved team Manchester City because of his ego!

Despite what he said in public, Mel never gave me a chance in the first team because I didn't fit his criteria as a 'shiny shiny' player who would jump through hoops for him. I wasn't the only player at the time to have the same opinion, but he got away with murder in the name of Manchester City.

The City period of my life contained some of the best and the worst times. I made brilliant saves and dropped expensive clangers. I gave my all for the cause and, I'll admit, it sometimes spilled over. A case in point was the home match on 5th December against Crystal Palace. This game often comes up in conversation when I get talking to City supporters about my time at Maine Road.

When it came to football aggression I have had my fair share on the pitch and in the tunnel. I knew how to look after myself. Playing with my brothers and mates at Manchester Apollo and Manchester City Social had taught me how to.

Mark Bright and Ian Wright started up front for Palace, and all afternoon they thought that they would bully and torment our players as they had a bit of a reputation as tough guys. Once or twice Bright had caught me as we challenged for the ball from set pieces which was fine, but then he went too far when the ref was not looking and elbowed me in the face in front of the Platt Lane end. Not a good move and, along with the fans, I was getting tired of Bright's antics. I immediately waited for my chance to get some payback and it didn't take long. A long ball was kicked downfield from the Palace keeper. It cleared my defenders and bounced towards me, chased by Bright. I accidentally left my elbow and foot in his face and he went down like Duke Street Bridge. I duly got sent off and Steve Redmond went in goal. We eventually got beat 3-1.

I took full responsibility for the defeat. I was a little naive but I got my point across in no uncertain terms, believe me. It was one of those moments when the red mist came down. However, by doing what I did, I had made my own issues bigger than my team's, and that doesn't fill me with any pride. There are very few regrets in my life about my professional football career, but I must say that one stands out.

There was another occasion when I got sent off at home against Palace. One or two of the apprentices watching from the North Stand told me that they feared the worst when I responded by ripping off my top and exposing my rippling muscles! What was going to happen next? Well, all I was doing was handing the shirt to my replacement!

The suspension that I received from the Mark Bright incident kept me out of two games in a run of 26 league and cup matches before Mike Stowell came on loan from Everton when I lost my place. It was one of a number of loan arrangements for Stowell in a relatively short period, but he never matched my record of all four divisions in one season! I don't think there'll be many more joining Tony Cottee and me in that exclusive club.

While he was playing at Maine Road, I was loaned out by City for the final time. In March 1988, I went to Tranmere Rovers. I must admit that I first thought that Tranmere was in Scotland – and to think geography had been my favourite subject at school! I soon realised that it was much closer. So it was that the Mancunian headed towards the Mersey. It was not a route that's been taken by many, with the two areas having such bitter rivalries on the pitch.

I knew that the club was in Division Four, but very little else. What I discovered was a beautiful place called the Wirral, a peninsula with the River Mersey to the east, the River Dee to the west and the Irish Sea to the north. It is about 10 miles long and seven miles wide, with views across the rivers to the skyline of Liverpool on one side and the magnificent mountains of north Wales on the other.

Tranmere was the only professional football club in the area and they played at Prenton Park in Birkenhead, not far from the tunnels which separated the Wirral from the city of Liverpool and Rovers' near-neighbours, the mighty Liverpool and

Everton Football Clubs. I played eight times for the first team, and during this brief period I made my second appearance at Wembley, in the Football League Centenary Football Festival, where we only lost one league match. The Wembley trip came about unexpectedly by virtue of the side's league performances between November and February. The fans scooped up tickets and the staff and spouses were treated to a weekend in the capital. This included dinner and dancing on the Saturday night, as it was expected that the team wouldn't get beyond the first day of the festival.

I wanted the regular goalkeeper, Billy O'Rourke, to play as I felt I did not deserve it. Rovers were superb, kicking off with a win over Wimbledon. The 'Crazy Gang' were on their way to winning the FA Cup that season, against Liverpool, so that was a major surprise. Dave Martindale scored the vital goal, in off Dave Beasant's post as I remember. On a weekend of surprises, we then faced Newcastle in the quarter-finals, having expected to take on Liverpool. Johnny Morrissey and Steve Mungall scored, I saved a penalty and we were through to Sunday and the semis!

There were a lot of Rovers fans who had to hastily re-arrange plans. The dinner dance happened, but it was an early night for us as we prepared for the game against Nottingham Forest.

Despite taking the lead twice through Ian Muir, the match went to penalties and we lost as Stuart Pearce finished it off. Yes, 'Psycho' can score from the spot! Forest went on to win the competition but, for Tranmere, it had been a fantastic weekend and we all left London hoping to taste the Wembley experience again. Little did we know how things would pan out over the next few years.

I was, of course, still a City player, and as I returned to the

City first team for the last match of the season, away at Crystal Palace, there were two things that I did not realise at the time. Firstly, that it was to be my last game for my hometown club and, secondly, that Tranmere Rovers and the Wirral were about to have a massive influence on the rest of my playing career. Incidentally, we lost 2-0 at Selhurst Park to finish ninth in the Second Division, and I 'broke up' for the summer without a clue about what was round the corner.

During the break, we visited the west coast of America for 16 days. It was a totally new experience for me, starting with three games in Canada. We then moved on to San Jose Earthquakes where George Best had spent a season some five years previously, scoring one of the greatest goals of his legendary career, while we also visited Los Angeles. The stadiums were geared to American football and part of our visit was to help promote a new football league in the States. Aside from that, the visit was a relaxing winding down exercise. A bit of sun, a bit of banter – time to chill. I was the only goalkeeper on the trip so had plenty of chances to get further match practice on the other side of the Atlantic.

One day, I got a phone call to say that we were signing a new keeper, Andy Dibble, from Luton Town. A few weeks earlier, Dibble had saved Nigel Winterburn's penalty in the 1988 League Cup final, in which Luton had beaten Arsenal 3-2 to claim their first major trophy.

It wasn't the best news that I'd ever had, but instead of me saying 'I'll give him a run for his money', I threw my toys out of the pram, got a bit cocky and left the club. I felt that I was the better keeper and if I had had a father-figure in the game to advise me at the time I could well have stayed and played many more games. I walked out as quickly as I had walked in on that Friday afternoon after work. Typical of me, the kind of impulsive reaction that had taken me in there had driven me out as well.

Looking back, I do feel that I could have become an even bigger name at Manchester City. However, now was the time to move on to the next stage of my career and my life. Despite some low moments along the way, it had been a very special experience to play for the club that I had supported as a kid. I got grief at times from the fans, but you could not ever doubt their passion for their club. They would turn up just to watch the grass grow if they could! It was time to move on, though.

There was a new challenge ahead, away from the city that I had been brought up in and the club that would always have a special place in my heart.

I will never be able to judge whether my career would have been more rewarding if I had stayed at Maine Road and fought to get the shirt back. What I was not to know, though, was that the next opportunity would take me back to Wembley on no less than six occasions, and that I would play a big part in taking my new club to its highest-ever league position. Added to that, family commitments were on the way!

Chapter Thirteen

A ROCKET RIDE BEGINS

'I could see potential at the club and wanted to be a part of it'

After my short period on loan, Tranmere Rovers had made it clear that they wanted to sign me. Johnny King had returned as manager towards the end of the 1986/87 season, his second spell at the club.

King was a brilliant gaffer and a fantastic person who was to teach me a lot about the game and about life in general, including the importance of having a good attitude and showing respect. It was clear that he wanted to include me in his team rebuilding although I think he was put off buying me because of the reputation that I had gained at Manchester City. It wasn't as a thug, a womaniser or a drinker, but as a person who wouldn't suffer fools and who looked after himself.

King did his homework and took a chance with a strong,

larger-than-life character because he knew what I was about and wanted someone like me in his squad. I signed in July 1988, age of 25, for a club record fee of £60,000. It was a massive boost to my confidence. I could see potential at the club and wanted to be a part of it. It was also good to have a clear idea of my position within the side, as number one keeper. King was obviously looking for a return on his investment and expected me to be the regular between the sticks for seasons to come. This differed a lot from the situation towards the end of my time at City, when I went through a period of doubt and a lack of confidence about my worth. Every mistake was being multiplied by the fans and it wasn't easy to cope with.

It was a new start, a clean sheet and I joined two relatively new signings to form the spine of the team. Jim Steel, a powerful striker, had been Rovers' record signing when they paid £50,000 to Wrexham in November 1987. He didn't have a massive amount of pace, but Jim more than made up for that with power and a good reading of the game. He never really wanted to be a footballer above all else. It was a means to an end for him and he was to become a policeman. Jim was a quiet fella with a dry sense of humour.

Jim Harvey had also been a record signing, this time for £25,000, when he joined about a month before Steel. He was a cultured footballer who knew his job. Jim made all the difference because he could calm things down. He would get his foot on the ball and use his vision and fantastic control to set up many a goalscoring opportunity. He used both feet and was lethal from set-pieces.

John King called the three of us 'the tree out of which the branches grew on each side' as the team took shape. For £75,000, Johnny King bought over 450 games and 66 goals from the two Jims and they were to play a big part in the Tranmere success story. I had been able to watch the two of them close-up during my loan period towards the end of the 1987/88 season, when Rovers finished 14th in the Fourth Division. It was a modest position compared to where I had come from, but I was excited about the challenge and believed that, under King, Rovers could quickly progress up the leagues. I moved to the Wirral straight away and have remained there more or less ever since. My children have been born there, and it is close to my heart.

I started the new season in good shape, eager to prove myself and repay the faith that Johnny King had shown in me. My form was good and the team started with three clean sheets, against Scarborough and Stockport County away, followed by Colchester United at home. The 1988/89 season was to be a triumph for the club and for me personally. I missed just one league match and made 59 league and cup appearances. The club finished as runners-up to Rotherham United and were promoted to the Third Division after 10 years at the bottom level. There were some great cup performances, particularly a 1-0 win against First Division Middlesbrough when Mark Hughes, who was to become one of my closest mates, scored a beauty with his head.

The overall attendances for home games rose from 76,396 in the previous season to 122,621 and Tranmere had begun the most successful period in its history. We knew we had to do more to build our hardcore of fans but there were two massive distractions for football followers just across the Mersey at Anfield and Goodison Park. The season ended on a high with over 15,000 spectators paying club record receipts of £42,652 as we clinched promotion against Crewe Alexandra.Hot-shot

Ian Muir scored the vital goal that gave us the point we needed, one of 29 that he had struck that season. We finished on 80 points, just two behind Rotherham. Exciting times had begun.

It was my first promotion-winning season, which gave me a great thrill and it was also a successful season for Manchester City, who went back into the First Division as runners-up, a massive 17 points behind Chelsea. Theirs was still the first result that I looked for, but I had moved on to pastures new and was really enjoying my football.

Prenton Park was quite different in those days with just the Main Stand surviving now from the structures that surrounded the pitch. It was a fantastic stand for its time, rebuilt in the late 1960s, and if you explore the rooms and corridors behind it today you will find many pictures showing happy and successful times at Tranmere Rovers. You won't have to look hard to find many a mugshot of yours truly, carrying a trophy while sporting a big grin!

Under the chairmanship of Peter Johnson, a number of extra facilities were added to the stand in the late 80s, such as the Tranmere Suite and the Dixie Dean Suite, named after the Everton goalscoring legend who started his career at Tranmere. Johnson was a Birkenhead lad, the son of a butcher, and his family business, based on Christmas hampers, grew so much that it turned him into one of the country's richest people by the early 1990s. He had been approached by Tranmere in 1987 after the club had run up large debts and he turned things round. Before his arrival, parts of the ground had to be closed to the public because they were in such poor condition.

As we ran out on to the pitch from the Main Stand, we would see open terraces on the other three sides of the ground. The Borough Road Stand was straight ahead with the Kop Stand to the right and the 'Cowshed' to the left. The 'Cowshed' dated back to the 1930s, when cover was provided for 5,000 spectators. It was soon christened 'The Cowshed' because part of it had supposedly come from a former farm building, and the name still sticks today.

The Prenton Park ground was hardly in the same league as the Anfields and Highburys of this world but it soon became home to me and I was to enjoy some fabulous matchday atmospheres over the coming years. Whenever I walk down the tunnel today, even when the ground is empty, I still feel the hairs on the back of my neck stand up.

It was around this time that I met Karen. We were playing at home one day when Ged Brannan came in to tell me that there was a policewoman who wanted my telephone number! You can imagine the banter that started in the dressing room and, naturally, I thought he was taking the mick! It turned out that she had been policing the games that I had been playing in and that she fancied me. You can't blame her for that! We started seeing each other soon after and it got to the stage where, if there was any trouble in the ground, I would tell her to stay where she was and not to get involved! Nico does have a sensitive side after all!

Karen's sergeant was a very good friend, Alan Boscoe, who has sadly passed away but he understood the situation and never put her in harm's way, that's for sure. Alan was always extremely pleasant and courteous.

Eventually Karen and I got married and I had two gorgeous children with her, Eric Junior in 1990 and Jessica in 1993. It was to be an up-and-down relationship but I will forever be grateful to her for bringing our two lovely kids into the world. As Eric and Jessica's mother, she will always be part of my life.

Back on the pitch, my run continued the following year when I made all 46 league starts. Striker Ian Muir was the only other player to do that. It was good to welcome my old mate from Maine Road, Neil McNab, although I was a bit miffed that they paid twice as much for him as they had for me! I was also not a happy chappy when Neil would say, 'Go and make the tea, sonny!' a reference to the time when he was a senior player above me at Maine Road! It was brilliant to play alongside him again, though. Neil was a great guy and a true professional.

I still had a serious attitude to fitness and training and it was paying off for me. I believed that I was the fittest player at the club and was always first up the sand hills on the Wirral coastline. I was getting runs of games that I never got at City, success continued for the team and attendances rose. Performances were good enough to take us to fourth place and qualification for the play-offs at the start of a love affair between Tranmere Rovers and Wembley Stadium.

Victory over Bury, 2-0 on aggregate, took us to Wembley Stadium for the final on 27th May but, a week before that, there was to be another appearance as we had also reached the final of the Leyland Daf Cup against Bristol Rovers. This trophy was designed to give more games to clubs in the bottom two divisions, and was played in regions during the early rounds. We had come through seven matches, finishing with a two-leg northern semi-final against Doncaster Rovers.

You can just imagine the excitement around the pubs and clubs of Birkenhead, Oxton and Bebington. Everywhere you went, Wembley seemed to be the only topic of conversation. The Wirral went mad as thousands of plans were made for not one but two journeys to London!

My first Wembley experience, the Full Members Cup with

Manchester City, had come and gone so quickly. I felt that I had been let down and isolated on the day by some of the senior pros around me. I was a raw, young professional, who lived a spitting distance from Maine Road and 24 hours earlier I had played the biggest league match of the season, the Manchester derby. The experience made me want to enjoy my second cup final and also think of others around me, particularly the younger players. I spotted a group of my mates before the match started and walked over to see them. I stepped over the barrier, had photos taken with them, then it was back over and into the game.

Bristol Rovers were the favourites. Managed by Gerry Francis, the club had just won the Third Division championship and had beaten Tranmere home and away. The weather was glorious and I made the best possible start with a double save denying Carl Saunders and Ian Holloway as early as the fourth minute. We then took the lead five minutes later when Ian Muir volleyed home from 20 yards out.

Bristol fought back and equalised just after half-time, danger man Devon White finally escaping from a young Shaun Garnett. They were threatening to take the game away from us at that point but I managed a couple of important saves before we got the winner on 71 minutes when Jim Steel headed past the Birkenhead-born goalkeeper, Brian Parkin. I was kept busy in the last part of the game but we held on for victory and I followed Jim Harvey up the famous steps to lift the trophy and receive our winners' medals.

Nearly 50,000 had watched the game, and even more Rovers fans greeted us back on the Wirral. We edged our way slowly through a sea of blue and white on our open-topped bus. We were followed by a cavalcade of cars, out of which trailed Tranmere scarves and flags, and the tooting of horns was non-stop! Children ran alongside the bus as we brought the Wirral to a standstill. I remember seeing people clinging on to any vantage point they could find – on roof tops and bus shelters, outside pubs. If there was somewhere to cling on to with one hand and wave a flag with the other, they found it! St James' Church was a popular choice, ideally situated on a roundabout. They even halted the bingo at the Plaza so that the punters could come out and watch us go by – eyes down became eyes up! You could barely see the Town Hall steps as they were covered in hundreds of scarves, flags and banners.

Eventually, we reached Prenton Park and I found a moment to get a picture of Eric Junior sitting in the Leyland DAF Trophy when just four weeks old!

My old mate, Jim Steel, would sometimes be on duty at the Town Hall when we came back from Wembley. We'd be up on the podium trying to get Jim up there with us in his policeman's uniform and the fans would chant his name when, in fact, it was us who'd won!

We hardly had time to gather our thoughts when we needed to start preparing for our next trip to London. Sadly, we were to taste defeat on this occasion, losing 2-0 to Notts County who had finished third in the league. In truth, we were a bit off the pace after the events of the previous week and Neil Warnock's side went on to bigger and better things.

Despite our disappointment, it was a memorable end to another great season for a club on the up.

Chapter Fourteen

LEADING THE WAY

'I was a very proud skipper as I led my team up the famous Wembley steps'

Success had come to Prenton Park, and there was no doubt that the players wanted more. It soon came – but not until there had been some legal wrangling over the summer over Swindon Town, who had been found guilty of breaking Football League rules. At one point, it seemed likely that we would begin the new season in Division Two and a second successive promotion, but things changed and we stayed where we were. A dream of footballing and financial glory was shattered: we had to dust ourselves down and start again.

The 1990/91 season began with a 2-1 victory at Bradford City, with Ian Muir striking twice, and it was a sign of things to come as, unbelievably, we ended the season with a carbon-copy of last time! Victory over Preston North End in the Northern Final took us to a second Leyland DAF appearance at Wembley, this time against Birmingham City, whilst a league position of fifth qualified us for a play-off semi-final against Brentford.

The two Brentford games were played in the week before the Birmingham match with the long journey south, fortunately, coming first. We drew the away leg thanks to a couple of goals from Steve Cooper and took the tie with a Ged Brannan goal at home four days before Wembley. Steve had recently been signed from Barnsley, recommended to John King by Joe Royle. He became one of my best friends at the club but, sadly, is not here today to reminisce over a few beers as he died tragically young in 2004 at the age of 39.

The Brentford success meant that lightning did strike twice, and we were in the fantastic position of back-to-back finals for the second season running. Waiting to meet us under the Twin Towers would be Bolton Wanderers.

In the Leyland DAF final, Birmingham had built up a two-goal lead by half-time but we hit back to level through Steve Cooper and Jim Steel. Unfortunately John Gayle would hit a spectacular goal for Blues – and six minutes later our defence of the trophy had ended. However, we had to re-group and start thinking about Bolton Wanderers in the play-off final. Between the two matches, we went back to Prenton Park for a week's training. We knew from the previous season that we had been a bit off the pace in the second final, and were determined to learn from that experience.

I was by now captain and the troops needed a rallying call. I stressed to the lads that the next match was the 'real deal'. I spoke to them as a group and individually. I was now the team captain, a senior pro and a record signing so I had to be a leader and show responsibility. I always remember Dave

Ewing, my old coach at Manchester City, telling me to 'roll my socks up and get out there'. This was a time to do just that. I demanded and commanded respect, and I also gave it back. I made sure that I was someone they looked up to, and these are characteristics which still carry me through today.

I spent time with the young lads like Ged Brannan and Shaun Garnett. No one asked me to do it, but I made it my job as skipper and leader. I told them all to get their heads up and to do it again for the supporters. I was better for it, and I think that they appreciated it. Like me, the fans knew that the next match was the big one, helped by a touch of rivalry that had developed between the two sides. Unlike our previous Wembley finals, this was a north-west only affair. The Bolton manager, Phil Neal, had really wound us up with remarks that he had made about Tranmere and we pinned them on the dressing room wall for motivation.

I made sure I was calm on the day, taking Joe Corrigan's advice on board. I stood in the goal and looked around the stadium. I took it all in. The first person who came into my mind, as ever, was my dad. His spirit was still alive – and always will be. Once again, I thought how proud he would have been of me. He would have been there, urging me on.

We lost Jim Steel through injury after 14 minutes and he was replaced by Chris Malkin, meaning a change in our game-plan. Bolton had dominated the early part of the game but, following the change, we got back into it. A Malkin header was disallowed in the 38th minute and, five minutes after the break, the same player saw a header come back off the crossbar.

Wanderers came back into the match and I kept us in the game with about 20 minutes left when I saved well from Julian Darby. Neither side was able to get the decisive breakthrough and the game went into extra-time.

Malkin, finally, did the business, controlling a rebound from their keeper in front of goal and hammering home the winner. Johnny Morrissey has given Ged Brannan plenty of stick since that day because Ged picked up Morrissey's through ball, which had been aimed at Chris Malkin, and tried the shot which led to the rebound, denying Morrissey an assist.

Chris attempted a forward roll and the fans went ballistic! There were chants of, 'We are going up!' for the rest of the game. Keith Hackett's duly whistle went and the party began! Don't ask me what time we got to bed, but I seem to remember the sun rising as we got back to the hotel...

Fifty-two years in the lower divisions had ended, and I was a very proud skipper as I led my team up the famous Wembley steps. John King summed up the success with one of his more easily understandable quotes: 'I always thought that there was room on Merseyside for three clubs'.

Looking back on that occasion, I have always considered myself very fortunate to have had the chance to lead a winning side at Wembley, but do not feel that I have been given enough credit for my role as captain. Much of the attention and many of the headlines, inevitably, went to Chris Malkin, and he certainly had a game to remember after coming on as substitute. But, for me, it is as if the game didn't happen at times. I look at the pictures and remember the joy we all felt, but I think that in lots of other teams the skipper would have got more credit because of who he was. Why shouldn't I have the acclaim? I put a lot of work in during the days leading up to the game, and on the day itself. I enjoyed the job and felt that it was making me a better all-round player.

Despite that gripe, there was no denying that the record

books would show that, counting the Football League Centenary Festival in 1988, Tranmere Rovers had taken their loyal supporters to Wembley five times in four seasons.

During the season I had been watched by Liverpool manager, Kenny Dalglish, as possible cover for Bruce Grobbelaar. The eccentric South African had come under criticism for his erratic style but Kenny could also have been influenced by my being English as the UEFA ruling for European competitions classified Irish, Welsh and Scottish-born players as 'foreign'. Kenny was keen to increase his English number of players in order to make an impact.

I wanted to play at a higher level again, and made no bones about it. Ideally, that would be with Tranmere Rovers and I didn't think that playing reserve-team football for another side would take me forward. I must admit, though, it was a big boost to my confidence to know that such a massive club as Liverpool was interested in me. I also remember reading a couple of newspaper reports linking me with Old Trafford. It must have been around the time that Sir Alex Ferguson signed Peter Schmeichel in 1991, and it was reported that he was interested in me going along as number two keeper. Again, it was flattering at the time but it didn't happen so that was it.

Throughout my career I heard and read rumours about clubs who might be interested in signing me, but it was never obvious whether you were being watched, or by whom. There would always be the scout in a flat cap in the corner of the ground minding his own business, but it was never openly talked about and there was never any point in getting carried away.

I was the only ever-present in the league during 1991/92 and, in fact, just missed the one FA Cup game through flu. This had given Paul Collings a chance, only his fifth appearance in three years, which showed how difficult it was for other goalkeepers at the club to get ahead of me. Paul's three-match run the previous season had only come about due to my suspension. He had never been on the losing side, and admitted that my consistent level of performance was making it very difficult for him to get a chance. John King recognised Collings' efforts, admitting that he would make many other first teams. Paul eventually left to continue plying his trade in the northwest at Accrington Stanley, Bury and Altrincham.

We established ourselves in Division Two and finished 14th, thanks in no small way to a shrewd signing by Johnny King just before the season started. The arrival of John Aldridge from Real Sociedad for £250,000 must have been one of the best bargains in football history. King had already tried to sign Aldridge as a 20-year-old during his first spell as Tranmere's manager, but the club could not afford South Liverpool's asking fee of £3,000! Aldridge eventually moved to Liverpool before trying his luck in Spain. Forty goals in 76 games represented a good return in La Liga but he was keen to get back to England and King pounced, eventually getting his 'gunslinger' for half the original asking price. Aldridge made his mark immediately with two goals in his debut game at Brighton, and went on to score a record-equalling 40 goals in all competitions – not bad for a 33-year-old!

The quarter of a million pound fee bought Tranmere 174 goals in 294 games, a club record beaten only by Ian Muir. He had an amazing following, particularly in Ireland. We went there a few times on trips and it was like travelling with the Pope! He was adored, and everywhere he went there would be autographs to sign and photographs to pose for.

Aldo went on to become player-manager and was truly a

Rovers legend, with a supporters' club named after him. I still see him today and he has become a good mate. Everybody talked of John Aldridge as being a hero but to be fair to him he never once talked that way or bigged himself up. Eventually I relinquished the captaincy and Aldo took over. I went into Johnny King's office one day and said that I thought it was affecting my game. I was big enough and strong enough to come clean about that. John Aldridge was my own suggestion, that's how it was. One or two might have doubted it but whatever anyone says, that is what happened.

After five Wembley appearances in four years, there was not to be a repeat this time but it did not prevent us from having one of the most exciting cup ties in the club's history. The Zenith Data Systems Cup first round home game against Newcastle United on 1st October 1991 was, on the face of it, just another match. It was a windy night, and the game was being televised. Our big-name opponents were destined to end the season below us in the league and the attendance on the night, 4,056, was modest by the standards that we had now reached.

It turned out to be a classic, and Sky Sports still show highlights some 20+ years later! The two sides traded goals, and the scoreboard kept rising. From Mick Quinn's opener for the Magpies after just three minutes, the game just leaked goals! A 3-3 scoreline led to extra-time, during which we looked to have sealed it with two more goals. Newcastle came back to level the scores before both sides finished with penalties to make the final result 6-6! Aldridge, as ever, was at the heart of things by netting a hat-trick.

I remember the subsequent penalty shoot-out as I saved kicks from Lee Clark and Liam O'Brien, while Quinn missed. We came through that 3-2. What a match! Aldo was furious when

I got awarded Man of the Match, as I went home with a mountain bike! Following that drama, we went on to beat Grimsby and Middlesbrough before losing in the fourth round at home to Nottingham Forest.

After a few dodgy results in the early part of 1992, Johnny King changed his system and signed Pat Nevin on loan from Everton. The move galvanised Nevin's career, and brought a new dimension to the Rovers team. The loan deal was to become permanent by the start of the new season, and the former Chelsea winger went on to gain 14 more Scotland caps whilst at Prenton Park.

I was enjoying my football and my form was good. I felt that the people on the Wirral wanted me, and that was exactly what I needed after not always feeling appreciated at Manchester City. I was also feeling pretty good about Merseyside as a whole when I became only the third Tranmere winner of the prestigious 'Liverpool Echo' Dixie Dean Award, given for services to football on Merseyside. The awards dinner, appropriately, was held at Prenton Park where the great Dixie started his career in 1923 with 27 goals in 30 appearances. I dropped the trophy, and said that I hoped that it wouldn't affect my England chances!

There had been talk linking me with the England team but I suppose it was always going to be difficult when you weren't in the top league. Neville Southall, the legendary Everton and Wales legend, was a big fan. Nev suggested that I was good enough to play for England and valued me at £2m on the transfer market. Neville and I had trained together for two seasons when I moved to Tranmere and in an interview with the 'Daily Post' he was very complimentary about me:

'I rate Eric very highly. He is without doubt as good as any-

'he Nixon boys: ack row (left to ght) me, Alan and eslie. Front row: .son and Philip

Big influences: Eric Senior (left), and my parents together (right)

Manchester Boys Under-11s: I'm on the back row, far right. Future Man City star Steve Kinsey is holding the ball in the front row, circa 1973/74

City days: Everton v Manchester City, May '87 – Mick McCarthy looking up, Neil McNab looking on. Below: Me and Alex Williams with goalkeeping coach Alan Hodgkinson

Record-breaker: (Left) In action for Southampton at Arsenal in 1986-7, the season in which I played in all four divisions

Suited and booted: Below: With some of the City squad on a factory visit, a week after a 10-1 win over Huddersfield in 1987. Left to right: Ian Brightwell, Kenny Clements, David White, Paul Simpson, Andy Hinchcliffe, me and Steve Redmond

Signing in at Tranmere: With manager Johnny King, July 1988

Wembley return: (Right) The open-top bus tour of the Wirral, May 1990

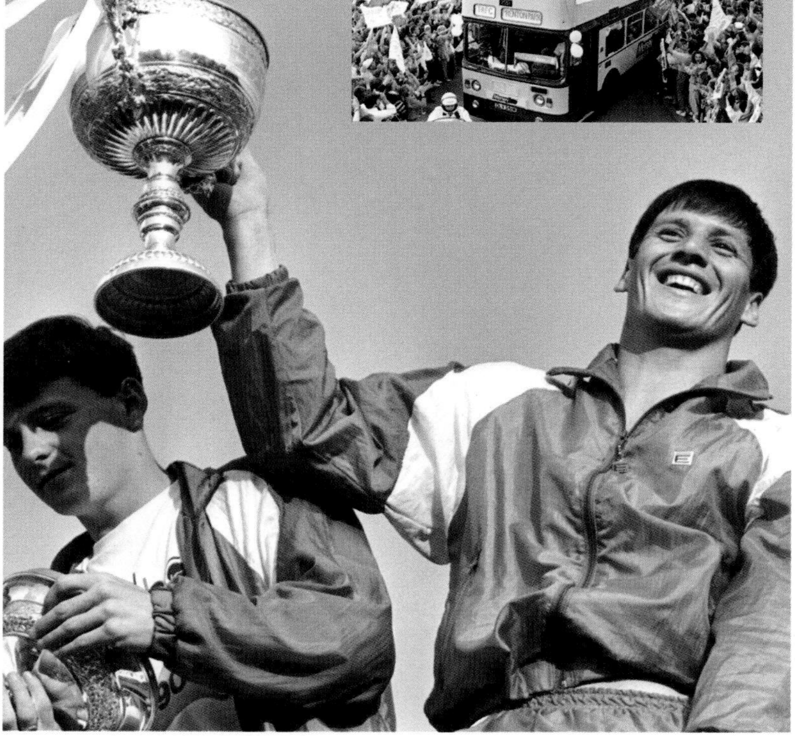

Lifting it up: (Above) Holding aloft the Leyland DAF Cup alongside Tony Thomas

Skipper: Celebrating victory in the Third Division Play-Off Final against Bolton Wanderers at Wembley, June 1991

Leyland Dad: Eric Junior celebrates in the Cup! Right: In Tranmere action, 1991

Pints all round: Enjoying a quiet night with Tranmere team-mates (from le to right) Neil McNab, Mark Hughes and the late Steve Cooper

Penalty king: (Above) Saving from Lee Clark during the victorious penalty shoot-out which followed an amazing 6-6 draw with Newcastle United in the Zenith Data Systems Cup, October 1991

White Christmas: Festive greetings from the Tranmere squad, circa 1991

Anglo-Italian relations: Exchanging pennants with Reggiana skipper Loris Dominissini, November 1992

Mind game: Deep in thought during the penalty shoot-out against Aston Villa, Coca-Cola Cup semi-final, second leg, February 1994

On the bench: (Above) Sandwiched between Tranmere Rovers boss John Aldridge and assistant-manager Kevin Sheedy

Shared views: In discussion with Tom Bennett at Stockport County

Testimonial: Saluting the crowd with Eric Junior, Jessica and Amy, 2002

Silver lining: (Left) Winning the Masters with Manchester City

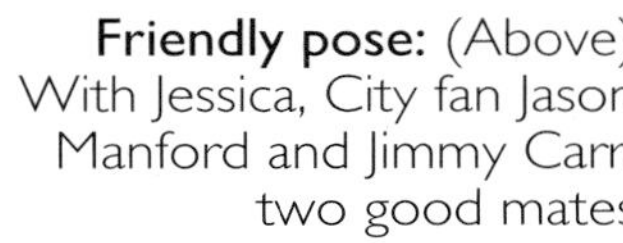

Friendly pose: (Above) With Jessica, City fan Jason Manford and Jimmy Carr, two good mates

Father and son: (Left) With Eric Junior at the Etihad Stadium

New boss: (Right) With Brian Little during his tenure as Tranmere Rovers manager

The King plays Prenton Park: Elvis back where he belongs – performing on the Wirral

Watching brief: (Below) Alongside former team-mate, Micky Mellon, manager of Fleetwood Town

The Nixon cla (Left to right) Jessica's friend Nikki, Jessica, Bradley, Nikki (Eric Junior's girlfriend), Eric Junior, Amy and Rachel

one playing in the top division. It was always his concentration that let him down. Now he is sharper and more focused. If he was a division higher he would be in the England squad.'

They were kind words from a master-keeper. Another big supporter was Harry Gregg, who had taken me to Carlisle on loan back in 1987, and there wasn't much that he did not know about goalkeeping. When we faced Watford in January 1992, their manager, Steve Perryman, had said pre-match that it was a battle of Britain's top two goalkeepers, David James and myself. The former Tottenham and England midfielder argued that to do the business in the lower divisions showed quality because they are the hardest in the world to play in. James had already been capped by Graham Taylor at England Under-21 level at that time. His next stop was Liverpool and, ahead of him, were over 50 England appearances! Johnny King recognised the amounts being quoted for him on the transfer market, but reckoned that he had a keeper who was just as good!

The nearest I had got to international honours was a call-up for the England 'B' team, which never happened! It must have been a couple of years previously. I was potholing in Ghyll Head in the Lake District and didn't get the message so Dave Beasant played instead! I was kept in the dark that day...

A few months after the Watford game I played for a representative Football League team managed by Glenn Hoddle, who was Swindon's manager at the time. We won 3-1 against an Italian League team and our ranks contained legends such as Andy Cole and Steve Bull. Other than that, the only other representative teams that I was selected for were the PFA Teams of the Season, selected by the professionals in each division. I was proud to be chosen for three consecutive years, 1988/89, 1989/90 and 1990/91, and think I had every right to be there. I got a lot of respect from within the game for what I achieved at Tranmere.

Rumours circulated linking me again with Kenny Dalglish, who was by now in charge at Blackburn Rovers, but they were defused by King who said that the majority of managers in the country would like me in their side, but unfortunately for them he was in ours! My name was mentioned in the media on a number of occasions as sides looked to cure a goalkeeping problem. I remember one piece suggesting that I was on Nottingham Forest's wanted list. Brian Clough had been critical of Mark Crossley and suggested he was a weak link as his side looked for silverware. Apparently, Forest representatives watched me as well as ex-Oldham keeper Andy Rhodes and Wolves' Mike Stowell.

I had already learned a lot about the game and the art of goalkeeping. On the one hand, I suppose I was always the showman, the crowd-pleaser. I would juggle the ball on my fingertip basketball-style and let the ball squirm through my legs and trickle over the line as the mascot for the day would try to beat me from the penalty spot!

I would never give my team-mates a break, having a go at them for not being able to put the ball past me in training. The likes of Muir and Morrissey would say that I was one of the hardest, most robust and angry people they have ever met on the training ground!

Then, when it came to the pre-match warm-up, I would be taunting them as I dived headlong across muddy goalmouths to stop stinging practice shots from Aldridge, Cooper and others. Once the game had started though my mind was focused, whether I was diving at feet or catching high crosses.

Earlier in my career, I was perhaps distracted too much and

the swagger often led to lapses in concentration. That side of my game had long since gone and a lot of credit for that is down to Johnny King. It meant that I was better-placed to make that one crucial save, which could turn one point into three. A typical example was against Plymouth Argyle in November 1991. It was a bitterly cold night and the score was goalless. I'd had little to do in the second half and my rocks were beginning to freeze solid when, 20 minutes from time, Argyle midfielder Mark Fiore got clean through. I raced out and blocked his shot with my knees. The ball ricocheted to a Tranmere player, and the ball moved quickly upfield where John Aldridge was brought down by Plymouth keeper Rhys Wilmot. Cue the soft-shoe Aldo shuffle, 1-0. Game over, another clean sheet, another solid performance. It was the sort of night that kept my confidence sky-high. I kept 134 clean sheets at Tranmere, just a shade under one every three games.

I knew that, injuries permitting, I was going to get runs of games stretching into seasons, and that helped confidence as well. The side were performing well week in, week out and there was a buzz around the area. The people at Tranmere wanted me and the fans wanted me. At Manchester City, I was young and inexperienced and playing in a team that was going through a lean spell. I never really got a chance and if you made a mistake you were dropped.

I was a great 'prowler', from side to side along the edge of my penalty area. My arms were often like windmills and my booming voice alerted defenders. I was probably more effective at communicating than many of the PA systems we came across! As a team broke forward, I would back-pedal to the six-yard box, crouch and be ready to spring into action. The closer the ball came, the more I would bark out instructions such as,

'Don't let him turn!' or 'Stand. Hold him!' If I was needed, the spring would unwind. At 6ft 4ins and a shade over 15st, I filled the net. Indeed, many shots seemed to come straight at me. However, I could also reach the top corners when I had to and many a striker has buried his head in his hands in anguish as I've stretched to turn a shot away from danger. Since those early solo gym sessions at Maine Road, I had always worked hard on my technique and it was constantly paying off.

I brought a different dimension to the team. Until then, Rovers had been used to their keepers booting the ball upfield. I made them aware of the value of a goalkeeper throwing the ball out, setting up many a move with my strong and accurate distribution. I continued to take training seriously, so much so that I would often end up in scuffles with my own team-mates!

I well remember a session before the Leyland DAF final against Bristol Rovers. We were concentrating on 'shape' and Johnny King would always go to an 11 v 11 game as he plotted the downfall of the next team. We played what we called 'shadow' football, in other words, non-contact. Stevie Vickers and Shaun Garnett were at the back when a cross came over. I went out to catch it and crashed into Eddie Bishop as he came in. I went for 'Bish' and threw a punch. At that moment, Shaun moved in to stop it and got a crack on his lip for his troubles as my punch hit him with some force!

Chapter Fifteen

THE SOCIAL SIDE

*'We would train hard, play hard and drink like f***'*

It wasn't just the level of football that made the Tranmere years memorable, but also the way in which the players got on off the pitch. I love a laugh as much as the next guy and, fortunately, I had found a team of mates who knew how to have a good time. Boy, did we party! There were so many characters in the team and we got away with so much that just wouldn't be possible in the modern game. We gave a whole new meaning to the phrase 'match preparation'! Our players gelled so well because they understood each other. They trained together, played together and drank together.

If you wanted a good laugh you need go no further than Johnny Morrissey. Johnny's the funniest man that I've met in football, nearly as funny as me! Muir and him used to be hilarious together – the Abbott and Costello of football. They were two of the biggest piss-takers at the club and would wind me up all the time. Steve Mungall used to call them 'Shit and Shite.' When they were both on song it was like stereo. They battered you all the time with their chat.

I remember how the double act used to rib me about my small calves. It became an in-joke and it amused them that a guy built like Charles Atlas, the famous body-builder, from the waist up could be so lacking in the back of the lower leg. There was a practice match on the Prenton Park pitch one day. Unbeknown to me, the lads had decided that when I took my next goal-kick everyone would run deep into the opposition half so that I couldn't reach them with my goal-kick!

A lot of Muir and Morrissey's banter was directed at Dave Higgins and Steve Vickers, who would sit across from them on coach trips. Dave and Steve were always together and we thought they were joined at the hip. There would be a running battle between the four of them for the last laugh, the final word. It was good value just listening to them prattling on, and it was never long before the next can was cracked open.

Some of the lads, particularly Kenny Irons and Ged Brannan, would have this 'sacrificial lamb' idea. I would go down to the back of the bus and one of them would take it on themselves to jump on me, threaten me, get a battering and then they would all beat me up. I would always say 'one of you is coming to hospital with me!'

While all the lager was swilling around and the 'effing and jeffing' was going on, Pat Nevin would sit quietly reading his books with a glass of orange juice. We would try it on with him but he'd just tell us to shut up so we did. Pat wasn't a loner by any means, but we respected his wish to leave him alone, and knew when to stop.

We loved a drink and on many occasions the booze would flow. Mark Hughes, Stevie Cooper, God bless him, and I would be 'hard school' with the likes of Shaun Garnett, Ged Brannan, Kenny Irons and Steve Mungall also never far from a can or a bottle. 'Mungy' reckoned he never touched alcohol until he was 30, but in the next five years made up for the previous three decades!

On one occasion, an away game was cancelled. I think it might have been at Watford. A few of us sat on the team bus and had three crates, then went out for a team meal, trying to make out that we hadn't been drinking! By this time we must have had 16 or 17 cans each, it gets difficult to count after a while! We sat Stevie Mungall at the end of the table, away from the coaching staff and Kingy at the other, as he was absolutely blitzed. We propped him in his seat and put a knife and fork in his hand. He had a stupid grin on his face all the time, but got on with eating his meal. Johnny King looked down the table at him and, at that very moment, the 'Lion of Prenton Park' landed face down in his dinner! We fell off our chairs laughing. Mungall was renowned for being a bit of a character, and he and Shaun Garnett would slag each other to death hour after hour 24 hours a day, then proceed to happily play alongside each other in the same team.

Actually, Shaun and Steve were best mates. Steve always said that Shaun's dad blamed him for leading his lad astray but reckoned, in fact, that it was the other way round. Johnny King called the two of them into his office one day. He told them that he had more letters in his drawer about them than the rest of the team put together. They weren't from interested clubs, but bannings from local boozers!

He told the pair that he had heard from the landlord of the

Caernarvon. They reckoned that they had been having a laugh and a joke when the barman says to 'Mungy': "Will you tell your mate to stop swearing?" Garnett relayed the message to 'Mungy': "Tell him to f*** off!" So 'Mungy' duly turned and indeed, told him to f*** off!

Steve regrets the day he took a hot spoon out of his cup of tea, and burnt the back of my hand with it! Revenge was needed so, on another occasion, there was a big pot of tea sitting waiting to be emptied. I got hold of a serving ladle, stuck it in the hot tea, pulled Mungy's shorts down and branded his arse!

I remember me and our physio/trainer, Kenny Jones, seeing Garnett off in New Brighton one night. No problem! Shaun's a lovely lad who, if he were a stick of rock, would have the words 'Tranmere Rovers' written right through him. He had joined from school, made 146 appearances and now works on the coaching staff with youngsters eager to make their way like he once did. You could pull his leg a lot, like the time he went out on loan in the 1992/93 season and the three clubs he played for were all to go down at the end of that season! Shaun came back towards the end of the season and was banned from our dressing room ahead of vital games!

I have always had a particular regard for Shaun ever since he made me and the missus a cup of tea when we looked around the club for the first time. He eventually became my boot-boy after I signed for Tranmere.

Well, back to the night in New Brighton. Shaun knew I'd be drinking pints and decided that he couldn't keep up with me so he went for Southern Comforts instead. After a time, I decided to join him on the Southern Comforts, as well as drinking pints with him. The club shut at two and Shaun tells of how he staggered home, was sick everywhere and then finished up shitting himself! He blamed me because if I'd left him on the Southern Comforts he would have been fine! Then he blamed his dog! Honestly, these young lads...they can't hold their drink!

A particular favourite haunt in Birkenhead was 'Ruperts' on Argyle Street. On a Wednesday night they would have a drinks offer – 50p a drink was certainly bad news! If we played on a Tuesday it would leave Wednesday free to get down there but even when we played on Wednesdays, we would still find time to take advantage of the offer! We would travel back and head straight down to Ruperts. There would perhaps be a dozen or more of us each time. When we went out we went in force!

Away trips were opportunities to indulge. One of the most legendary was the time when we travelled to Southend in 1994. We had beaten Bristol City at home on New Year's Eve, and were due to play on January 2nd in Essex. Knowing what we were like, the manager didn't want us celebrating the New Year before the Southend game so we set off straight after the Bristol game. Johnny King did not make many mistakes, but that certainly was one. He should have known better!

We smuggled some Budweisers and bottles of wine onto the coach and had a meal of fried rice, or some such, on the coach on the way down, before stopping at a massive pub where Kingy decided we would have a couple of quiet drinks, let the bells in for New Year then head off to our hotel. Slowly but surely the boys started disappearing until there were only about four left. Kingy asks Norman Wilson, the club secretary: "Where are the boys?"

"They were here a minute ago' the answer came back. They walked around the back of this huge place, where they found a full-blown disco and the boys giving it plenty on the dance floor! Kingy orders Norman, who is quite a character himself, to: "Get them on the bus!"

We got to the hotel at about half 11, and the gaffer told us to get to our rooms to drop things off and then straight back down to see in the New Year. The dance floor was full, there was a black-tie do in full swing and we soon got involved! Above the dance floor was a net full of balloons. At about two minutes to midnight, Ged Brannan pulled the chord and all the balloons started falling to the floor. That was the cue for everyone to start singing Auld Lang Syne! Two minutes later, Big Ben sounded!

One of the fellas at the function had obviously primed the guy on the disco that he was going to propose to his girlfriend as the New Year began. You can just imagine the banter and stick that we gave him! Our lads were trying to drag him away, telling him not to be so crazy. 'Don't do it, mate!' He resisted, and made a young girl very happy. But I often wonder all these years on whether they look back on that night and remember a group of drink-filled, crazy young men from the north-west, trying to sabotage his romantic moment!

The boys then went into the bar area where Kenny Irons asked Ronnie Moore what time the curfew was. "One o'clock" was the reply. So one o'clock comes and goes and Ronnie is asked again. "The gaffer says two o'clock." Well, that was Johnny King's second mistake of the trip!

Anyway, it got to about three o'clock and we were still knocking it back. Ronnie Moore started winding me up, saying that the manager was going to sack me. Ronnie, a former player, was now on the coaching side and would eventually have a stint as manager. As a player, he started as a centre-half before making a successful switch to striker. Well, the more I drank, the more I took the bait! Eventually, I stood over Ronnie and threatened to throw him through a plate glass window, as you do! I kept urging him to "get up, get up!" out of his seat, but I must have terrified him so much that he stayed glued to his chair for the rest of the night!

Things died down a bit but then I remember sitting on a chair in the foyer minding my own business when Ged Brannan suddenly rushed up to me, knocked the chair – and me – over and started play-fighting with me and Irons on the floor. Suddenly, I felt a crack on the jaw. It was Johnny King, who had suddenly decided that he did not want to miss out and chinned me! I retaliated and, as the others got off me, I stood up and launched Kingy away across the floor. Unfortunately, his head hit the corner of the bar and blood started pouring out! I hadn't done it on purpose, but he didn't look pretty.

Ronnie went over to Steve Mungall and told him that the gaffer wanted to speak to him. His eye was a real mess, and the blood on his lips looked just like lipstick. He had it all over his shirt as well. Mungall just started laughing.

"It's no laughing matter" said Kingy, "what am I going to do with Nico?" Steve replied: "You've smacked him. We were just mucking around and you came over and smacked him. You can't do anything!"

"Am I supposed to let him off?" the reply came back.

"You'll have to because it's your fault!" insisted Steve.

The manager went to hospital for stitches, and came back with a great big blood mark. From that day he was christened 'Gorbachev'! I think it was Dave Higgins who coined that nickname – it was a bad cut though.

So there we were, down south. We had deliberately set off when we did so that the lads could not drink too much, and at three in the morning everyone was smashed! The guy who had made the decision to leave early and avoid the distraction of the booze had been to hospital! We eventually got to Southend, and still came away with a point after a 0-0 draw. The journey back to the Wirral was nearly as eventful as the one going down! Ged, Kenny, Kenny Jones and I got through 96 cans of lager. All in all, that was quite a trip!

We would always drink on the coach on the way back from games. We would slip the driver, dear old Albert, a fiver and he would bring out a case or two of lager from the baggage area underneath. Good man! I'm sure Albert dreaded taking us at times. One night he was driving us back along the M62 in snowy conditions in December 1990 after, I seem to remember, an FA Cup tie at Scunthorpe which we lost 3-2. God knows how we got the game played, and I know that loads of fans had trouble making the match and getting back. Anyway, Albert parked up at a service station for a Jimmy Riddle. He had gone off to the toilet, when I decided to liven things up by moving the coach. I got in the driver's seat and drove it round the corner – I loved the big steering wheel! Albert came out...no coach. For two or three minutes he was demented. He eventually went round the corner to find me standing by his pride and joy with a broad smile all over my face!

We also liked our nights out on the Wirral and in Liverpool. It would usually be Thursday, Friday and Saturday, and I would never miss a session. At times, things would spill over and a fight would start. One night we were in 'Rubber Soul' on Mathew Street near the 'Cavern'. It was a players' night out and the England v Italy game was on the television.

There was a guy in there who was giving the lads stick for different reasons. Stevie Mungall, born north of the border in Bellshill, always wore his heart on his sleeve. He was at the front shouting for Scotland! The guy said sarcastically: "You lot got a great result today." I think Scotland had drawn 0-0 with Lithuania, and Steve replied: "Aye, you're not kidding. What a great result that was for us!" The guy kept chipping away. Ged Brannan was going to chin him at one point. Anyway, Italy scored and Steve jumped up, shouting: "You beauty!"

Moments later, a chair came over from further back and split Danny Coyne's head open. All hell broke loose. Well, I was not having that. I copped sight of the lad and pushed some bouncers out of the way to get through to him. I picked him up by the scruff of the neck, got him on the floor, gave him a whack before kicking him out of the door. He wouldn't do that again in a hurry after I'd finished with him!

We would certainly hammer the beer, as newly-signed John Aldridge was soon to find out. Just after he joined Tranmere in 1991 we played at Brighton. We pulled up at about eight o'clock in the evening and had our usual meal. After the long trip, Johnny King let us relax with a couple of pints. A group of us – there would be Kenny Irons, Ged Brannan, Ronnie Moore and Kenny Jones – went looking for Aldo and asked him if he was coming to the pub. "You're having a laugh, aren't you!" was his reply. The legendary striker was used to stricter regimes in Spain and at Liverpool, and soon found out that we weren't. We knocked the ale back between nine and 11 o'clock, our preparation for a match the next day! Aldo liked a pint but, to be fair to him, he was more restrained than many. He had played for one of the biggest clubs in the world and was idolised by the fans. He took this role seriously. I always looked out for him because, as a high-profile figure, he would attract the attention of a minority of idiots and he knew that I was a bit of a fighter who could look after myself.

I suppose I was protective of all the players in the squad. I was a big guy who could look after himself, and felt a responsibility to be there for my team-mates and to look after them, just as I had been with my brothers as we grew up, likewise with the apprentices at Manchester City.

We got into a regular drinking routine. Whether we were playing in Nottingham, Cardiff or London we would arrive on the coach early evening, perhaps have a swim or a bit of a stroll, eat a meal, then walk it off – in the direction of the nearest boozer. The regulars would be me, Ronnie Moore, Mark Hughes, Kenny Irons and Kenny Jones. Some would join us for a quiet pint or two, but would never batter it. It was good to calm the pre-match nerves.

Five or six pints later we would get back to the hotel for a night-cap in the bar. Johnny King would be happy for us to have a drink in the hotel before games, so we did. Often he would stand on sentry watch back at the hotel, but we would push one or two of the younger lads through the front door and come in through the kitchens. The next day he would tell us all: "I know exactly who was out, where you were and how much you had to drink. If you don't perform today, you're dropped." He was saying, 'You've crossed the line, now you've got 90 minutes to put it right.' More often that not we went out and did the business. We knew we wouldn't ever let the fans down and if drinking had ever become a problem, we'd have done something about it. The gaffer wanted us to enjoy ourselves and we did, perhaps carrying it further to extremes than he intended. Nevertheless, we had success on the field despite that. We would train hard, play hard and drink like f***.

King knew what we were like when we got going because he had seen it for himself in Magaluf. The players would often holiday together and a favourite place was Magaluf, the holiday resport in Majorca which is popular with Brits. It had all we wanted. Plenty of sun, nice beaches and loads of bars and nightclubs. We would be up by about half nine in the morning then it was straight to the beach, where we would knock back the lagers until about half six, then we would race back to the hotel to see who could be first into the pub dressed. If you took longer than five minutes you were fined. We often ended up in the Piano Bar, where tourists used to get up and sing. My party piece was 'Living Doll' by Cliff Richard and Eddie Bishop would do his Elvis. That got me really started!

I remember one Magaluf trip when Bish had gone over convinced that he was going to win the karaoke competition. There we were in Pickwick's Bar. 'Bish' did his bit, and I followed. It went to the audience and I won! I think the lads will tell you, particularly 'Bish', that they never heard the last of it. There were to be many more nights when I was to go on stage and bash out a few songs...

A young kid in the group, who had better remain nameless, got arrested one year and thrown into prison. We had to pay to get him out. Then there was the time me and Aldo got on to one of those big bungee steel bars that fire you into the air. Well, the two of us nearly shit ourselves when we realised what we'd got ourselves into. It was worth it though to see the look of terror on his face!

'Super Duper' Stevie Cooper, Mark Hughes and I would go abroad regularly. I remember one trip where we went on an all-inclusive holiday to Spain with our families. After about three days the guy in charge told us not to come back again because we had drunk the place dry!

As I've said, Mark was a really close mate, but his musical

tastes were really beyond me. His liking for The Communards stretched the friendship at times! In fact, his taste in music was about as good as Steve Mungall's dress sense. 'Rag and bone' Mungall was an absolute nightmare. It was never good to see him standing next to Jim Harvey, who was quite the dapper guy by comparison.

As for Dave Higgins, well his sense of humour and dress sense were so offbeat, we nicknamed him 'Spaceman!' Higgins was mad and extremely funny. He would come in one day with brown hair, and the next day it would be orange. At Christmas parties, he would let the fire extinguishers off. He would walk through his room and then come down saying it wasn't him, yet there would be a trail of frothy footprints behind him. Dave was forever a practical joker. He'd put his hand up at a meal and when the waiter came across, Higgins would pretend to scratch himself under the arm.

We trained hard but lived life to the full, and I was never far from the centre of things. There was one period when both Aldo and I were suspended from the game. In John's case it had been as punishment for the infamous attack on the match officials in the 1994 World Cup, when he and manager Jack Charlton became heated as they felt that Aldridge's appearance as substitute was being delayed.

We were as thick as thieves, and went off to the Isle of Man for a few days. We would get as drunk as skunks and come in at all hours. We were in the lift one day and standing to our right was none other than Johnny King – He got everywhere! The gaffer had tracked us down and fined us a week's wages. Kingy used to call Kenny Jones and Ronnie Moore his sheepdogs when he wanted us rounding up! In truth, those two were as bad as anyone. Kenny Jones could give me a run for my money, while Ronnie was not far behind. Teacher's pet, though, was definitely Ian Muir. We called him 'SOG', which stood for 'Son of Gaffer'!

Aldo was a passionate guy who always wore his heart on his sleeve, whether as player or manager. I well remember one occasion when we were playing Norwich City at home. I was coaching at the time. One of our young players was getting caught on the ball too often and being bullied by a City player. Our guy was well over six-foot himself, and played centre midfield, but hadn't had many first-team games by then. He told Aldo that the Norwich player was treading on his feet and pinching him. Aldo, Kevin Sheedy and myself were pulling our hair out on the touchline, telling him to get physical and look after himself, but it just wasn't happening. Aldo told him to get stuck in and retaliate – wait until the referee's not looking and punch him! If you don't get a chance, wait until after the game in the tunnel. We had endured enough of this by the end of the game and said to him, 'We'll make a cordon round you and you can lamp him!'

The lad finally caught up with him in the tunnel and it all kicked off, big style. All 22 players got involved in what is a tight area at Tranmere. There's not enough room to swing a canary, never mind a cat! The Norwich player went down, before getting up like a bottle of pop about to explode. Two stewards, knowing my reputation for fighting in tunnels, grabbed me so that I could not move. I was trying to shrug them off, when one of their players comes in over the top and pokes his finger into my eye right up to the first knuckle!

The situation calmed down and Norwich assistant-manager, Doug Livermore, came out to complain. Aldo was telling him to get his biggest man out, and that we'd sort it out. Suddenly I hear Aldo shouting: "Nico, out you come!" I had an eye that's swelling up, I'm lying on the physio's couch with a bottle of Optrex and he's shouting, "Go get him, Nico!" Cheers, mate!

Another funny moment involving Aldo was a game at Birmingham one Tuesday night. For some reason, Aldo and Ian Bowyer started having a row on the touchline and it didn't take much to light the blue touch paper with Aldo! As goalkeeping coach, I was close to the action. Half-time comes and Aldo's waiting for Bowyer. I have a quite word, he calms down and heads for the dressing room as he doesn't want to get fined and be handed a touchline ban.

Throughout the second half, I spent most of my time stopping Aldo from killing Bowyer! The game finishes and Aldo is waiting for Bowyer by his dressing room door; by now he is fuming and he wants blood – Bowyer's blood. Bowyer walks into Aldo's vision and the shouting and cursing starts for about five or 10 minutes, with me in the middle. Finally, the situation calmed down and Aldo walked into our dressing room, only to hear Bowyer shouting down the corridor: "You were a shithouse as a player anyway, Aldo!" Well, you can guess what happened then. Round two, and the rest is history.

You could fill a separate book from all the reminiscing we do when we meet up. That was something that I never experienced at Manchester City. I remember one of the Tranmere lads likening us to slabs of meat in the end. We come and we go. The game moves on after we have left it, and it is up to us to fulfil our potential while we have the chance. That is all you can do – and that is certainly what we did!

Chapter Sixteen

ITALIAN JOB

'I remember Johnny King bending down to kiss the ground, just like the Pope'

The 1992/93 season brought us another 'first'. We played our first competitive away game in a European competition when we took part in the Anglo-Italian Cup. The Tranmere fans were suddenly reaching for passports, booking flights and buying all the Italian dictionaries from WH Smiths in order to learn some lingo! The competition took place from time to time between 1970 and 1996, and had been started up again in for the start of that season. It was to be for clubs in the second tier of football in the two countries.

We qualified by beating Wolves and Peterborough in a group stage, then played four games against Italian teams. Our first trip took us to Reggiana, a city in the north of the country between Milan and Bologna. A charter flight left Manchester and on it were 120 paying supporters as well as the full squad, directors and management. There was a hairy moment when the stewardess wrongly announced that we had arrived in Boulogne, and I remember Johnny King bending down to kiss the ground when we arrived, just like the Pope! Many other supporters had found ways across to Italy and there were some great tales to tell, including the coach driver who had to stump up to pay for an on-the-spot speeding fine!

Pat Nevin chased a thief to recover a stolen camera on behalf of a supporter, and we overcame language barriers with the help of a Wallasey pizzeria owner who worked on Radio Merseyside! The match was far more forgettable than the activity that surrounded it.

We won our first game on European soil a month or so later at Pisa, in the shadow of the Leaning Tower! To be fair, there weren't many shadows as torrential rain hammered down. There were two games at Prenton Park, one won and one lost. In the end, Derby County pipped us to a semi-final place, but it had certainly been an experience.

Just before the competition ended, we entertained West Ham United on Friday, 4th December. Friday matches were not uncommon as we tried to avoid clashes with one of the 'big two' across the Mersey, and they became a more regular feature at home. There were some great nights and it seemed to give us more publicity, with goal highlights being shown the following day on 'Saint and Greavsie'. I remember this particular match against the Hammers because not only did we win 5-2, but we also went to the top of the First Division! John Aldridge, the master marksman, scored a hat-trick and described it as his best Tranmere moment.

My fifth full season with the club had brought yet another good run of games, with 45 league appearances and 14 in various other cup competitions. Rovers finished fourth in the league, their highest-ever position, and within touching distance of the top flight. Yet again, the play-offs were on the horizon with fifth-placed Swindon Town facing us. After losing 3-1 away, we came so close to making it to Wembley again, but a 3-2 home win was not enough in front of 16,000 fans. The club who had given us hope of promotion a couple of years ago, only to be reprieved for their wrong-doings, had, once again, got in our way.

The following season, 1993/94, saw even more success with a good run in the Football League Cup leading to a semi-final against Aston Villa. The first leg was at Prenton Park, watched by over 17,000. It was one of those special electric nights on the Wirral and, after 90 minutes, our fans were beginning to make plans for yet another trip to Wembley.

Johnny King made some changes in tactics which threw Villa's pre-match preparations. Instead of expecting Johnny Morrissey and Pat Nevin to come at them down the wings, the gaffer went with a 5-2-3 formation. We took the lead after about five minutes and it was Ian Nolan, yet another King purchase from non-League, who scored from 12 yards. Until then, the young full-back had been more used to entertaining the crowds at the Marine club up the Lancashire coast!

Villa were unable to respond and we kept sweeping forward. It was one of the quietest halves I've had, and I watched on as we set up chance after chance. The second came after 23 minutes and it was Mark Hughes who scored it after coming up from defence. Prenton Park was going mental! I didn't have to earn my corn until the 50th minute when I got behind a shot from Tony Daley. At last, Villa started to play to their reputation and we came under the cosh a bit. John McGreal did enough to turn a Dean Saunders strike wide, and it was all hands to the pump! We survived and went down the other end and scored a third. There was some doubt about offside, but John Aldridge did the business once again!

We were in injury time when Villa came back into the tie as Dalian Atkinson scored from close range. To make it even more frustrating, the referee apologised to Johnny King after the match as Chris Malkin had been fouled in the build-up. We had definitely deserved to go to Birmingham with a three-goal lead after the manager had surprised Ron Atkinson with that change of tactics – but we just had to get on with it.

Over 40,000 watched the return leg, and Villa clawed their way back to win 3-1 after extra time to leave the aggregate score at 4-4. The match went to penalties – and we lost, simple as that. I've still not been able to watch it to this day. We were then defeated in our next two league games, against Grimsby Town and Barnsley, but a run of five wins and a draw in April took us to fifth place and, yet again, the play-offs! Sadly, we missed out again. Leicester City held us to a 0-0 draw at home, then beat us 2-1 on their patch. The second leg will always remain in my memory for the wrong reasons and, once again, you can see the action on YouTube.

Leicester took the lead four minutes from the end with substitute, David Speedie, credited with the goal. Having already missed out in the League Cup semi-final, frustrations boiled over in injury time and one of our guys went down in a tackle. Everyone came together in a brawl, and I decided to get a piece of the action. I knocked down Leicester's Simon Grayson, who hadn't done anything, and ended up being dismissed along with David Speedie, who was then suspended for the final. It was a dramatic end to the season and one of those occasions that loads of fans still remember when they think of myself. However, if you are full of passion and fire and your mate gets hurt, you jump in and come to his aid. That's what happened with the Speedie incident, and it wasn't the only time in my career.

I was never one to hold back, and I remember a game against Portsmouth where one of their strikers had given me a dig during the game. Kenny Irons had got into a bit of bother with one of their players in our 18-yard box, and I acted as peace-maker. Their guy got a sly rabbit punch in on me and the referee got in straight away. I told the Portsmouth player that the referee wouldn't be there to protect him when the final whistle went. There were only about 10 minutes to go and, just as a referee can do when he knows he's had a shocker, so this Portsmouth guy edged closer to the tunnel as the end of the game approached. Anyway, the final whistle went and he was off like a flash with me after him, all set to knock seven bells out of him! I ran straight into Pompey manager,Terry Fenwick, and Terry Venables, who was working with him, stopped me from going any further. I shouted what I was going to do if I got hold of him, and he went straight home in his kit. I'm still waiting for my chance!

Due to my suspension following the Leicester incident, Danny Coyne began the 1994/95 season, playing in the first five league games. I then played 41 consecutive league matches, topping 40 starts for the sixth consecutive season.

For the second time, we took part in the Anglo-Italian Cup, with matches at Atalanta and Lecce. The Lecce game attracted just 286 spectators to a 55,000 capacity stadium. Once again, there were many tales to tell and I remember a lively trip back from Atalanta, including entertaining the party with the old favourite 'Living Doll'!

Without a win, we finished bottom of our group – but not before the Prenton Park fans had the chance to see two future world stars on their doorstep, Christian Vieri and Oliver Bierhoff. Having already faced Tranmere for Pisa in the previous competition, Vieri played for Venezia and went on to star at the very top of club level for teams such as Juventus, Inter and AC Milan. He also scored nine World Cup goals for Italy in the 1998 and 2002 finals. Bierhoff played for Ascoli and went on to score 37 times for Germany, including two in the final of Euro '96 when they beat the Czech Republic.

The Anglo-Italian Cup was abandoned after just one more season, largely due to fixture congestion. It has attracted much criticism over the years. It proved to be an expensive experience, and relationships between the two countries were frequently tested on the pitch, with bad blood between the sides.

On a positive note, it gave our fans a chance to experience Italian football and culture, and it gave them time 'close-up' with the players. It was also another chance to have an away-day piss-up! Hughesy, Cooper and me were often the scallywags. I remember when we played at Pisa the manager told us to go and have a cup of coffee and a bit of a relax. Mark Hughes and I got a 24-pack of lager each and sat near the Leaning Tower knocking the ale back. Take it from me, by the end of the afternoon that tower was standing absolutely straight – and I was the one leaning.

Chapter Seventeen

FRIDAY NIGHT FEVER

'I trained, slept, played, got changed and never saw them again'

A measure of the club's success was the quality of player they could attract. John Aldridge was a classic example, and Pat Nevin had been lured across the Mersey from Everton in 1992. Another to arrive was former Everton and Rangers defender,Gary Stevens, who moved from Scotland for a fee of £350,000 in September 1994. This equalled the club record, a figure that had risen nearly six times in the six years since I had put pen-to-paper to become the club's record signing myself. The England international went on to make over 120 appearances during the next four seasons, before retiring to study for a degree in physiotherapy at the University of Salford.

Signing the likes of Aldridge, Nevin and Stevens helped to make the match experience at Prenton Park that much more special for both the players and the fans. The decision was made to play a lot of our home games on a Friday night. We needed the crowds, and had to avoid Liverpool and Everton clashes on Saturday afternoons. Our home record was good. Prenton Park became a fortress and we beat all the big teams there. Playing the night before other clubs also gave you a jump start on all the teams around you in the league, which often happened because we had a good record on Friday nights. However, this move was not always popular with visiting teams, and it got to the stage where they would not play us because they felt it gave us an unfair advantage.

Fridays became like the Mardi Gras. We couldn't wait for those games because we believed we were unbeatable. The floodlights would illuminate the 12 or 13 thousand in the ground,and then the show began! Nevin would be at them down the left, Morrissey down the right. Muir and Aldo scored goals for fun. Hughesy and I bossed things at the back, Dave Martindale and Harvey the midfield. We played pure, cultured football from the back line to the front. It was no kick and rush, route one stuff for us. Sometimes we would play with wing-backs – the likes of Stevie Mungall and Mark McCarrick. This was a new idea at the time, and many teams just couldn't cope with it. I still remember the time that 'Crackers' scored with his arm in a sling. He was a real character, although he did regret pouring a bucket of iced water over me at a Christmas party!

Very rarely did we get beat at home. We got on the pitch, did the business and then it was upstairs to the lounge for some bevvies, where the post-match celebrations would begin. Friday matches were popular with the lads because they got a few beers on the night and then had the weekend off. The fans would join us, and the hospitality suites under the Main Stand would be heaving. It was their chance to chat with their footballing heroes, and they loved it.

Job done, I always enjoyed lounging around on a Saturday, watching the other results coming through. By then we would have made arrangements for a night out, usually in Birkenhead. We might go to Charing Cross and Ruperts, then on for an Indian. That wasn't just because we needed some food, it was also a chance to carry on drinking.

I got to know many of the regulars in the hospitality boxes, partly because I was usually one of the last to leave. One of them was a guy called Keith Nethercott. I had already got a connection with Keith because his kids, Lewis and Holly, went to the same school as my Eric and Jessica. Keith had a thriving glass company on the Wirral. Despite being a Liverpool fan, he supported Tranmere Rovers and he and I got to know each other so well that he eventually became one of my best men when I re-married! Keith was a generous fella who loved a laugh as much as the next man, and we were to share many of those over the coming years.

There was one time when he and I were in a group of 22 lads from the Hoylake area who went skiing in France. I was still playing football at the time, and going down mountains on skis was strictly forbidden. Although the club knew I was going away, they didn't know where. We had a whale of a time. I was a beginner on the slopes, but more than made up for it 'off piste'. Our rooms were like a disco every night, and we supped huge amounts of duty free that we had bought on the way. The unbelievable thing is that nobody at the club found out about it. I can't see that happening today with Facebook, YouTube and Twitter!

On a more recent occasion, Keith and I were part of a gang that went to Portugal to support a golf event organised by Vince Earl. Vince played Ron Dixon in the long-running Channel 4 soap 'Brookside' for 13 years, and was a Tranmere Rovers fan. Well, we were minding our own business having an evening meal when a well-known former player started to tap me on the back of my head each time he went past our table. I quickly reached the point where enough was enough and threatened that, if he did it once more, I'd knock him out. Sure enough, he did it again on the way back, and ended up with two black eyes and eight-or-so stitches.

Back at Tranmere, success also came off the pitch. After the Taylor Report forced a move to make grounds all-seaters, a new version of Prenton Park opened in March 1995. The Kop, Cowshed and Borough Road stands were demolished and replaced by three new stands. Ray Stubbs, who spent five years at the club before moving on to earn fame as a TV presenter, jointly opened the new development and there was a record attendance of 16,377 for the Middlesbrough game, our last league match of the season before the play-offs.

After a promotion in my first season, the club had gone on a remarkable campaign which resulted in five play-offs in six years. For the third successive season, we had given ourselves a chance of reaching the top flight. Having been second on April 14th, we faltered on the run-in to finish fifth and faced second-place Reading. Losing 3-1 at home in the first leg gave us a mountain to climb and we never made it, despite holding Reading to a goalless draw in the second leg.

The season saw the last matches for two of Tranmere's greatest servants. Ian Muir bowed out at home to Grimsby in March after becoming the club's all-time scorer with 180 goals in 393 games. Chris Malkin followed at the end of the season, having scored 75 times in 304 games. They were – and still are

– legends on the Wirral, and two of the reasons why the early 1990s was a great time to be a Tranmere supporter.

The club record was broken again in August 1995 as Shaun Teale came in from Aston Villa for £450,000, having scored against us in the League Cup semi-final the previous year. Teale joined a club boasting more international players than ever before, alongside products of the youth system who were coming through to the first team, and credit was due there to Warwick Rimmer. Although born in Birkenhead, Warwick never played for his home-town club, but turned out for Bolton and Crewe on nearly 600 occasions as a defender.

Warwick re-established a youth policy at Tranmere which had been abandoned in the 1980s because of a lack of finances. Despite competing against much bigger clubs in the area, the system has netted the club millions of pounds as players of the calibre of Ged Brannan, John McGreal, Tony Thomas, Ian Moore and Jason Koumas have moved on to higher levels.

My old club, Manchester City, bought Brannan for £750,000 in March 1997. As well as being great company, Ged was a quality player, playing either in midfield or defence, who made over 300 appearances for Tranmere and was involved in the build-up for the goal which defeated Bolton Wanderers in the play-off final in 1991.

John McGreal headed to Ipswich Town for £650,000 in 1999 after making 233 appearances for Tranmere. John was a brilliant central defender, who had been a floor tiler before getting invited to come to the club for a trial. He and Shaun Garnett formed a strong defensive partnership.

Tony Thomas, another product of the YTS scheme, was a superb attacking full-back who made 314 appearances and scored the quickest goal ever by a Tranmere player – after

7.7 seconds against Southend in 1991. 'Tank' made the short journey across the Mersey to Everton in 1997 for £400,000.

Ian Moore, son of Ronnie, went to Nottingham Forest in a million pound deal in 1997 after making an impact with his goals and assists, while West Bromwich Albion bagged Jason Koumas, the skilful playmaker, for £2.25m in 2002, a figure which was to be Tranmere's record sale.

This was a phenomenal record for one club, and represented some brilliant business deals. As for Teale, his stay was shorter than expected and he was allowed to leave on a free transfer with only 62 games in the Tranmere shirt.

After over 400 games, I missed out on the 1995/96 season as Danny Coyne was ever-present. I had helped develop Danny since he was 15, when Warwick Rimmer had asked me to take him out on to the Prenton Park pitch and assess him. I was still player and skipper at the time. Danny was not the tallest of goalkeepers, but he was a very good one. I could see the potential in him and I like to think that he learnt a lot from me over the years. He got his first international cap for Wales in 1996 and played 16 times in all. With Danny in possession of the Tranmere jersey, I went out on loan twice. In January 1996, I joined Reading and in February, I played for Blackpool.

The Reading experience was a strange one. They were at a loose end and needed a goalkeeper. I had played against them a number of times for Tranmere and was happy to oblige. I signed for a month, but the deal had a 24-hour call-back clause in it. I joined the team on a Monday night as they prepared for a League Cup quarter-final at Leeds United. I trained, slept, played, got changed...and never saw them again! Tranmere had activated the 24-hour call-back button and I went back to Prenton Park! I must say that the Reading players were a good set of lads and I was glad to help out, albeit briefly. We lost the match 2-1, by the way.

Almost immediately, I headed north to spend about three months at Bloomfield Road. Blackpool were in Division Two at the time and the fans scented promotion. I did not even know what position they were in but my mind was made up by the fact that Sam Allardyce and Phil Brown were in charge. Phil was a good friend of mine. We had been the opposing captains when Tranmere beat Bolton at Wembley, and I had great fun reminding him of that! I also needed first-team football and Tranmere did not want me to go on loan to another club in Division One. As for Sam, well he no doubt wanted me not only for my goalkeeping ability, but also for the fact that I had a lot of experience of end-of-season promotion pushes and play-offs with Tranmere.

Big Sam had got a fantastic atmosphere going around the club and had splashed the cash with the signing of Andy Preece from Crystal Palace, following the arrival of Andy Morrison from Blackburn and Tony Ellis from neighbours Preston the season before. Mind you, once I got there, the gaffer soon stopped Preece and Ellis practising their shooting on Fridays because it destroyed their confidence when I had everything in my pocket! I saw it as a personal affront if anyone scored past me in training, let alone in a game – I hated getting beat!

In amongst the squad was a certain Micky Mellon, and he and I were to meet up again at Tranmere Rovers and develop a great friendship which, 12 years later, took me to Fleetwood Town – but more of that later. I was drawn to Micky because, like me, he was as straight as a die. Mind you, he will always regret the night he went out with Andy Morrison and me!

I am good friends with Andy now but for some reason he

must have seen me as a threat when I went to Blackpool. We were similar characters. We were both strong, robust and wilful. Dave Linighan and I went out one afternoon for a few drinks in town. It got to about six and Andy and Micky joined us. We had a few more jars and it got to the stage where me and Morrison were like a couple of raging bulls banging heads. I felt Morrison was a bit of a bully who thought he could get away with murder. Well, he couldn't with me.

At the end of the night something happened between us and we went outside The Savoy and started brawling. Micky tried to get between us. Andy went one way and I went the other. The police arrived, and Micky ended up getting arrested! It was funny really, and we still mention it to this day. I wind him up by saying: "Come on, don't be giving me any trouble now!" Seriously, he's a great mate of mine is Micky, and a player who was very unlucky not to play at the highest level. Incidentally, after the incident with Andy Morrison, I seem to remember turning out with a black eye in Blackpool's next game!

Blackpool had gone top and were looking cast-iron certainties for promotion. We were winning plenty of games and I was having a good time. Unfortunately form dipped at the wrong time, and we ended up in the play-offs – an experience that I was well used to by that stage in my career. We made a great start against Bradford City, winning 2-0 away, but things went badly wrong in the second leg and we lost 3-0. City went on to win promotion.

For some reason, I took the brunt of the flak for the defeat. I had played well during my 20 or so games and been a part of the success. This view was backed up by things that I had heard years later when working back in the area at Fleetwood. I admit that I might have been at fault in the play-off second leg. Their guy lobbed me on the first goal and I made a mistake – but none of us played well. I felt harshly treated. It was a disappointing end to a fantastic time on the Lancashire coast. I had made some friends for life. Times were usually good off the pitch and, as usual, I enjoyed the social side and the banter.

I believe that Big Sam had tried to buy me while I was there, but Tranmere refused. In the end, Sam also headed off down the M55 having paid the price for not achieving promotion. The setback did not halt his progress and he went on to achieve lots of success, particularly at Bolton Wanderers. A great guy!

I headed back down the M6 to find Rovers struggling for form. The chairman, Frank Corfe, had appointed John Aldridge as player-manager assisted by Ray Matthias and Steve Mungall. Johnny King was moved to the position of director of football after masterminding the greatest period in the club's history and, quite rightly, having the Borough Road stand named in his honour in 2002.

Confidence was low and a 6-2 thrashing at Derby County had been a sad end to the gaffer's time as Tranmere manager. He was both realistic and sad about the decision:

"I have put my heart into everything I have done at this club but you have to be big enough to take these things in football because it's the most lethal game in the world. This job has been my life and I feel I have a lot more mileage left in me. That's what hurts."

Aldo felt a dilemma between his loyalty to King and his own ambitions to go into management. The immediate reaction to his appointment was a run of six games unbeaten to the end of the season and a final position of 13th in Division One. The 'gunslinger' continued playing for a couple of years, but his appearances became more and more limited. His final emotional appearance was at home to Wolverhampton Wanderers on 3rd May 1998. Typically, John scored the two goals that won the match and he became the club's oldest player in a league match, until one E.Nixon was to pass that record!

Danny Coyne kept his place as Rovers began the 1996/97 season with a 1-1 draw at Southend. I packed my bags once again and set off down the open road, this time the M62, in the direction of West Yorkshire. Life is full of twists and turns and here I was, four months after facing them in the play-offs for Blackpool, pitching up at Bradford City on loan!

I had done my UEFA 'A' Licence at Lilleshall and came across Chris Kamara, known to all now as a Sky Sports pundit, but manager of Bradford at the time. He asked me if I was interested in getting a few games under my belt, and I went back to Valley Parade in September 1996. It had been 10 years since I had last played there and it had not been the happiest of times for me. But I was now 34-years-old with some points to prove and I wanted to regain my confidence after the play-off experience that had gone sadly wrong at Bloomfield Road.

I appeared in 12 games and played well, winning a number of Man of the Match awards. 'Kammy' had a good team at the time with the likes of Gordon Cowans and Chris Waddle. They were talented footballers and were, of course, riding high after their promotion the previous season. Also, Gordon and Chris were two examples of many nice people who I have met through my footballing career. It makes me laugh now to see Chris Kamara on Sky Sports. He is still as he was then, a great guy and a jovial kind of bloke – Nothing's changed! Chris would do anything for anybody.

Once again, Liverpool were interested in me, this time to go to Anfield as cover for first-choice goalkeeper David James. Joe

Corrigan had phoned me on behalf of the club and came to watch me. The attention certainly improved my performance. I was heading across the Pennines as Bradford were at home, to Palace, I think. The phone rang. It was an agent that I had been connected with for six months or so. I was surprised to get the call because, until then, I had not heard much from him. He was supposed to help but he didn't. He talked a good game, but his actions didn't match up.

The guy talked about the interest from Liverpool and, suddenly, the old Eric came out. I told him that he had done nothing for months and now, all of a sudden, the money had started talking and he wanted to be involved. I told him what I thought. I told him straight. I said to him:

"I'm not being funny mate, but where have you been in the last six months? Can you smell money or something? Beat it, and don't ever phone me again."

I told him to get off my back as I was not interested in him and what he stood for. If I had bitten the bullet and gone with him I might have become a Liverpool player. I really believed that. Not for the first time, my direct honesty had won the day, and left me wondering what might have been.

My trips to Bradford and, later, Sheffield, were often made by motorbike. I enjoyed riding by bike, and still do. However, there was many a winter's day when I would arrive for training in full leathers but with hands red raw. They are massive goalkeeper's hands, which took a long time to thaw out!

There was one occasion when I came off in frosty conditions at about three in the afternoon, and the bike was spinning round and round in the middle of the road. A tanker was bearing down on me and I had to make a quick decision. I got up quickly, moved the bike out of the way and the tanker missed me by about six metres! If I had not done what I did, I wouldn't have ridden that bike again!

I was coming to the end of my career, and I had lost my position at Tranmere to a very promising keeper who was the face of the future. I felt that a move to Liverpool would have been the pinnacle of my achievements. I would have been happy to start on the bench but, believe me, I was still competitive enough, and fit enough, to make the first team. Age was no barrier. I had always kept myself in shape, and had a good track record over the years. I had never accepted days off, and two replacement knees are proof of the strain that I constantly put my body under. My answer to every situation was to work harder – and I eventually paid the price.

It is one of those lessons learnt and something I make sure that I pass on to young players today. When they are left out, their first reaction is to want to run around the block and do everything harder and faster. That's not the answer. It is better to take stock and work through a plan with the coach.

I played 12 games at Valley Parade before returning to Prenton Park and a run of 25 league games to the end of the 1996/97 season, in which we finished 11th in Division One. The old order was changing, and familiar faces from many shared experiences were no longer around. Muir and Malkin had departed in 1995 and, before that, my great mates Steve Cooper and Mark Hughes had also gone to pastures new. Cooper had been signed by York City for £30,000 in 1993, and Hughesy went to Shrewsbury in 1994. Dave Higgins moved on to Barrow in 1997 and Johnny Morrissey signed off against West Bromwich Albion in May 1999.

Chapter Eighteen

A NEW CHALLENGE

'I needed eleven stitches in the cheek so, as you can imagine, I was not in the best of moods!'

Seasons come and seasons go. Fans' expectations at the same time each year as they come out of the summer break, confidently predicting big things for their teams. Bets will be placed, the latest strip bought and fixture lists scanned. The mounting excitement gets to the players as well. They can't wait to get back playing again. New signings will eagerly look down the programme to see when they will be playing their former clubs. An eye will also be cast to the end of the season. Who will be the opponents on the last day, and what will the team's situation be by then?

The 1997/98 campaign was now approaching fast. Pre-season had not been without incident. We played Everton in a local derby at Prenton Park. Just before half-time, their Scottish striker and notorious hard-man, Duncan Ferguson, lunged at a loose ball and put his studs into me. For good measure, he then came down with a right hook which connected with my ear. Naturally I wasn't best pleased with the big man, and we traded a few blows before the referee separated us. I spent most of the rest of the half jabbing my finger at him, threatening: "I'm gonna get you!"

Well, the whistle goes, and Ferguson legs it down the tunnel. I chased him from the goal area and caught him just before the changing room, where I pinned him against the wall. All hell broke loose around us, although I did not come out for the second half. We were lucky to escape red cards and if it had not been a friendly game, then we might not have.

Soon after this incident, Tranmere took a phone call from Stockport County. County were riding high after just gaining promotion from Division Two but manager, Gary Megson, did not have an experienced goalkeeper. They offered me good money in a £110,000 deal, which wasn't bad for a 34-year-old. Tranmere did not appear to need me, and any approach from Liverpool had come and gone. I moved back to the Manchester area in August 1997.

Paul Cook joined me at Edgeley Park. Paul, like me, was the wrong side of 30, but Megson understood us as people and what we could offer. Cooky had been bought from Coventry City for £250,000, and was one of Johnny King's last signings. He was at the club for about 18 months but played around 60 times. He was a natural left-footed player and a great passer. He didn't get forward a lot, but could read the game well. Five years later there was a place for him in the Dream Team that I selected as part of my Tranmere testimonial celebrations.

I had a great time back at the club against whom I had made my mark in front of Manchester City manager, Billy McNeill, all those years ago. We finished a respectable eighth, which included wins at home to both Tranmere and City! I can honestly say that, even though the move had taken me by surprise, it was one of the best seasons that I have ever had, playing in a good team and for a manager who I have huge respect for.

Gary Megson had just arrived at Stockport from a spell as manager of Blackpool. He has taken stick over the years from certain quarters but, for me, he was a fantastic gaffer. He was an honest bloke who was always straight down the line and, as you will no doubt have gathered, that's how I like it. Gary was a man's man and a man's coach who had played at the highest level with Sheffield Wednesday and Manchester City, and I will always be grateful to him for giving me a chance.

He also treated us like adults. I remember one Tuesday just before Christmas. We had just played a match and I wanted to go to New York to do some Christmas shopping. Gary let me go on the condition that I was in Manchester again by Friday!

Being back in Manchester was a large part of making the season such a good one. I loved the Wirral, don't get me wrong, but problems had developed off the pitch and it was good to not only get away for a while, but also be back near my roots. Things were not going well with Karen, and our relationship could be volatile. The move put some distance between us, but it also meant that there were a number of practical issues to overcome regarding the children when they visited me. Christmas was certainly difficult, but you just got on with it.

Karen had gone skiing to Aviemore around April time and a letter came through my door filing for divorce. Despite our problems, this was the first I knew about it and it was the day we were due to play Manchester City at Maine Road! Suddenly, I had to sort the kids out before going to work in front of 30,000 spectators. Eric and Jessica would have been about eight and six at the time. I took them to my mum and showed her the letter. It was as much of a surprise when she read it as it had been for me.

It wasn't a good day at the office. City won 4-1, and I did not play particularly well. My cause was not helped in the first half when I had to leave the field after I had received a kick in the face from Shaun Goater. I needed eleven stitches in the cheek so, as you can imagine, I was not in the best of moods!

Overall though, there weren't many days like that and I will always be grateful to County for a great time amongst good professionals and lovely people who helped take my mind off my personal problems. I played 46 league and cup games, but it was to be my only season for the club. In August 1998 I was on the move again.

My old Tranmere mate, Ray Mathias, was manager of Wigan Athletic at the time and had Roy Carroll in goal. It was suggested that someone of my experience would be good to have on the bench so I went to Springfield Park. Some 15 years earlier I had gone there for trials and looked in awe at the legends around me. Here I was again, but this time giving out advice based on the experience gained from hundreds of league games. Wigan signed me permanently on a free transfer in March 1999. Despite enjoying being at County, I had fallen out with the board at Stockport over my contract and I decided I was too old to bother so I left. I managed three games for the first team at Wigan and fitted in yet another trip to Wembley when the side won the Football League Trophy, a victory that I watched from the bench.

It was soon time to move on for both club and player. As Wigan headed for a magnificent new stadium and a bright future, I had to face up to the reality that wear and tear was catching up with me and to be honest with myself about what I could cope with. My knees were not in good shape, following the rigorous training over the years, and injuries were beginning to become more obvious. I also had to have some work done to realign my much-used fingers. I was still training hard nearly every day, even as a coach. It was time to cut down.

Aldo offered me the chance to go back to Tranmere as full-time goalkeeping coach in July 1999. I had been one of the pioneer goalkeepers to take my FA 'A' Licence along with the likes of Steve Sutton and Alex Williams. This had involved a week at the National Sports Centre at Lilleshall in Shropshire and assessments for about a year. Big names such as Joe Corrigan and Peter Bonetti were also seeing it as a way forward.

I had always seen myself as a student of the game and became increasingly interested in the thought of coaching my specialist position. I felt that I had what it took to be successful. Having a coach supporting me was something that would have helped me considerably in my career, particularly the early years, but that was behind me now and I was ready and willing to use my experience to benefit others. I returned to Prenton Park eager for the new challenge which lay ahead.

Tranmere had signed John Achterberg on a free transfer from Eindhoven. John was to become my 'guinea pig' and I like to think that I made a major impact on his career. He was a similar character to me. He wanted to be the fastest, the strongest, the most outspoken – all traits you needed as a keeper, otherwise you would get left behind. He had not enjoyed the best of pre-seasons, however, and had a real problem with communication. This was often the case when you signed a foreign player, with the language issue sometimes being a barrier. John's way of giving information to midfielders and defenders was more like a conversation rather than short, sharp and clear directions, and this was something that we devoted a lot of time to over the weeks and months.

We also worked hard on technical aspects such as starting positions, coping with the ball played over the top and how to manipulate the game to our advantage. John was a raw product at the time and we had our differences of opinions, but we got on well once he and others at the club understood that I was no longer the former Rovers goalkeeper and captain back to claim my place.

John had been signed as cover for Danny Coyne, who had just regained his place following the sale of Steve Simonsen to Everton. The Dutch-born player proved to be a very agile keeper and a good shot stopper, making over 300 appearances in 11 seasons and twice being voted Player of the Season. His biggest disappointment was missing out on the Worthington Cup final against Leicester City in 2000 as Aldo went for Joe Murphy, another of my pupils. Joe had come across from Ireland as a young kid in 1998. Tranmere was his first club, and I was to play a big part in a career that led to over 300 matches for various clubs, mainly Scunthorpe United, and two Republic of Ireland appearances in 2003. I was proud of the fact that Joe, along with Danny Coyne and Steve Simonsen, all went on to gain international honours having benefited from my experience at Tranmere. Simonsen, like Murphy, had come to Tranmere at an early age when things had not worked out at Nottingham Forest. He was to play around 300 games, 166 for Stoke City, and gain England Under-21 honours.

A fact often overlooked at Tranmere is that, with Warwick Rimmer's help, I brought three future international goalkeepers through the ranks, which meant that the club did not have to shell out for a goalkeeper for years. All three have modelled themselves on my best features. They have watched and understood how I trained and conducted myself as a leader and a senior professional, as well as the role I played off the field. That explains a large part of why they have each gone on to become a stalwart at other clubs around the country, playing at the highest level.

John Achterberg, my 'guinea pig', has since become a goalkeeping coach himself, describing his move to Liverpool in 2009 as a "dream job" in the 'Liverpool Echo'. His role was involvement mainly with the reserves and youth teams, and gave him the chance to pass on many of Nico's wise words – as well as his own!

Before the 2000 Worthington Cup final, I decided to video the build-up to a match that once again captivated the attention of the Wirral supporters in the way we had a decade ago. It was the club's eighth appearance at Wembley and well-deserved after a cup run that had seen off the likes of Coventry City, Middlesbrough and Bolton. For three days or so I followed the action and filmed it. I was there in the hotel, at meetings and walking around Wembley the day before the game. It would be a memory for me, but part of me also wanted the players to see it to help them understand the occasion. I knew that, eventually, they would.

As a coach at Prenton Park, I wanted the players to appreciate the culture and attitude that had made Tranmere such a successful club all those years ago. I was a link between the old and the new, and it mattered to me that what we had achieved all those years ago was not lost.

I filmed Aldo giving his final team talk in the dressing room and followed the teams down the tunnel and on to the pitch. I captured the fireworks, the national anthem and the Royal Box as Rovers prepared to play in front of their biggest audience ever, with over 74,000 at the ground and around 300 million worldwide. A lot of people have asked me about the video over the last 10 years and one day I am sure that I will release it. The idea was to sell it to the players but this never happened, although my old mate, Steve Roper, did watch it recently. Martin O'Neill's Leicester City became the last team to win the League Cup at the old Wembley Stadium. We came back into the game after having Clint Hill sent off, but went down 2-1. Agonisingly, Scott Taylor hit the crossbar with a header in the closing moments.

The result, though disappointing, did not dampen the enthusiasm of the Tranmere faithful, who revived memories of the glory days as thousands gathered in Hamilton Square, after which there was a reception at the Town Hall in Birkenhead.

John Aldridge had got into trouble with the FA after clipping the ear of the Leicester substitute who laughed and applauded the sending off. This was typical of his passionate nature, and not the only occasion on which he and trouble came together.

Chapter Nineteen

KINGY'S HEROES

'We all looked after each other, protected each other and were shaped by the maestro'

I knew that I had to produce the goods when I arrived at Prenton Park back in 1988, and I did just that for 10 years. I was the first name on the team sheet and felt privileged every time I ran out and applauded the loyal Rovers fans in the Cowshed. I also played every game as if it was my last. Johnny King eventually gave me the added responsibility of being captain and I took this on board one hundred per cent. I knew that there were people out there who doubted me following the ups and downs of life at Maine Road and I desperately wanted to prove myself for the sake of the manager, the club and my family.

I captained a winning side at Wembley and became the first Tranmere Rovers skipper in Europe, leading them in the Anglo-Italian Cup. During my time, the average gate rose from 3,300 to over 8,000. Suddenly, the Wirral was on the map and the place to be!

As a player, person, father, husband and man I did it all at Tranmere. I gave everything on and off the pitch and the fans realised that. I was an asset on both the playing side and the commercial side of the club. I made it my responsibility to take the lead at Christmas parties and always had a word for those who worked at the club. It costs nothing, doesn't it? I perhaps wasn't everyone's cup of tea at times. I was confident and cocky, with a larger-than-life ego but that was all part of my success as a player and as a leader and the fans lapped it up.

I was pleased and proud to be part of a fantastic squad, and we still meet up. Get us together for five minutes and we're still nattering five hours later. They were special times and we never tire of re-living them.

In fact, we've launched a Former Players' Foundation with Steve Roper as chairman, and Neil Johnson. My wife Rachel and I came up with the idea and I'm acting as the liaison officer. I did a lot of research and looked at what other clubs are doing now, particularly Everton. The first event, appropriately, was held at Aldo's at Prenton Park. I arrange for players to attend functions in aid of charity and we raise money that will help former Tranmere players who have fallen on hard times and need money to pay bills or have a hip replacement.

There were many reasons for starting the foundation. One thing we wanted to do was re- create the type of spirit that was around the hospitality suites at Prenton Park after those Friday evening games, when players and supporters got together and partied into the night! We wanted to bring ex-players back to Prenton Park to meet the supporters again and reminisce at social events. Too many of them had left the area and begun new lives elsewhere.

When I joined the club I was quickly made aware of the players who had gone before such as Alan King, Barry Dyson and John Manning. I was fortunate to be part of a generation of players who helped drive Tranmere through its most successful period, and it was important that we kept their exploits at the front of people's minds. As well as satisfying the needs of the fans who had experienced it with us there was every chance we could attract new fans to the club.

Up to now, Tranmere Rovers have not been completely behind the scheme, which is a shame. They've accepted it but I wouldn't say that they have ever been fully in bed with us. I had a meeting with Peter Johnson, who was the chairman who made a difference all those years ago. I talked about the association that we were forming and I told him that we were not looking for money from the club but would appreciate some support. I think that there needs to be more give and take for players who put their careers on the line for the cause, and who fought together through everything. We had the same team for 10 years, which shows the loyalty we gave. We were loyal to the club and to Johnny King. We cared. Now we'd like the club to show that they appreciate our commitment. I gave my knees and fingers for Tranmere Rovers – and others are the same.

At the moment they won't allow us to use the club badge and name. We have to be known as 'Tranmere Former Players' Foundation'. We can't take the word 'Rovers', which is a bit frustrating. Hopefully this will change. The ex-players want it to happen, and so do the fans.

The former players have a great time when we get together and look back. We meet and re-tell it as it was. There will be Ian Muir, Jim Harvey, Kenny Irons, Chris Malkin, Stevie

Mungall and others, all swapping yarns. We get 20 or so ex-players together over a few drinks, just like in the old days, and we talk about how we put Tranmere Rovers on the football map. We talk about the Wembley trips, Italy, how the money and success attracted players of the calibre of John Aldridge. We remember with pride how we turned Prenton Park into a fortress, and smile as we think back to all those fantastic Fridays.

The fellas talk about the teams we beat. We defeated them all at one time or another – Chelsea, West Ham, Fulham... In some ways we were a team of misfits who gelled under the Svengali-like figure of Johnny King. Many other managers had tried but admitted defeat and released the players, only for them to be signed up by the gaffer and become stars because they all got on and understood where each other was coming from. By today's standards we didn't have a big squad and often relied on a group of 15 players or so as well as occasional players such as Kenny McKenna. Kenny, a forward, was a bit of a local hero and played his football for a range of lower league clubs around the north-west. He went on to score stacks of goals at Altrincham and Conwy United.

We would remember Steve Cooper, who sadly passed away all too early. Steve scored two great headers in the play-off semi-final with Brentford in 1991. He was a bit of a gymnast as a kid and had a famous back flip to celebrate goals. Limited in ability, he went on to get most of his recognition at Airdrie but he was second-to-none as a guy and a family man. It was so sad when he died at his home in the Midlands aged 39 because I lost one of my closest friends in the game. Stevie is one of many who have carved a special place for themselves in the history of Tranmere Rovers.

At the heart of the success was Ian Muir. Unbelievably, Ian was signed by Rovers manager, Frank Worthington, on a 'free' in 1985! He travelled up from Brighton where Worthington had first come across him, and he had seen a bit of the Stan Bowles swagger and show in him. Worthington decided that he would sign him if he ever had the chance.

Muir had made just a handful of appearances for five different clubs over the previous five years and was transformed, particularly under Johnny King, into Tranmere's all-time top scorer. As much as Aldo was to do the business on many later occasions, Ian Muir scored the goals that mattered at the time and was simply one of the best strikers that I've ever seen. Within five seasons, Ian had beaten a club scoring record that had stood since 1935! His goals played a massive part in getting the whole success story rolling and, to this day, I don't think he gets the credit he deserves. He had silky skills and was a deadly finisher. His latter career at Tranmere was affected by a cruciate ligament injury picked up against Chester and he moved on as the club found another deadly marksman in the form of John Aldridge.

Many Tranmere supporters saw Ian Muir as the second Messiah and, to me, he was right out of the top drawer. The fans only got to see him on a match day but we had the privilege of watching him display his talents each day in training. He was a brilliant trainer. If he was pissed from a night out at Ruperts club in Birkenhead on the Wednesday he'd still be the best trainer on the Thursday!

The club also got great value from another prolific striker, Chris Malkin. 'Stick' was working for Barclays Bank and playing local league football when Johnny King invited him to Prenton Park in 1987. Chris couldn't give up his job straight away, but signed as a professional the following year. Following a free transfer, Tranmere took on a guy who hit 75 goals in 304 games, and who was then sold to Millwall for £400,000.

Chris enjoyed a drink but was one of the quieter fellas, compared to the likes of yours truly. He would do anything for you – he'd catch pigeons for you or chase a paper bag across the pitch! He would be the first to say that he was limited as a player but, boy, could he score you goals. I would never back myself in a 100 metres race against 'Stick' because he could shift. He was very much in the mould of Peter Crouch, without quite having Crouchy's ability with his feet.

Then there was John Morrissey. After unsuccessful periods at Everton and Wolves, he became one of the finest wingers outside the top flight and right at the top of the long list of great wingers to have graced Prenton Park. Nobody would have Frank Worthington at the top of their all-time managers' list but he could certainly spot a player. He was responsible for 'Mogsy' signing for about eight grand just two months after Ian Muir had made his debut. Morrissey had genuine pace that skinned many a defender, and he supplied an endless number of pin-point crosses for Muir, Malkin, Aldridge and others. I didn't play with a better winger in my career. Mind you, he'd get my vote every time as the worst trainer – he hated it!

Just for good measure, Worthington's short reign as manager also saw another significant signing as Steve Vickers was brought in after impressing with non-League Spennymoor. Frank gave him his chance at centre-half and he set the ball rolling, but it was Johnny King who took Steve to greater heights when he paired him alongside Dave Higgins and Mark Hughes. Steve never got flustered. He always stayed on his feet and was a steady influence.

Mark Hughes was another who had not set the world alight before joining Rovers. He had been used to being a man-marker but did his best work as a sweeper under Johnny King, while Dave Higgins and Dave Martindale had played for King before and were his first signings. Higgins had been with the gaffer at Caernarfon Town.

Mark 'Crackers' McCarrick was yet another unsung hero. His longest spell had been at Lincoln City, during which time he had witnessed the tragic fire which killed 56 people in a stand at Bradford City in May 1985. Having started by sending his CV to Johnny King, 'Crackers' was at Tranmere for four seasons and could always be relied on to give his all. He impressed the crowd with a brand of tackling and a gung-ho approach that went down a treat on the terraces.

Eddie Bishop was recruited from Runcorn in 1987. Eddie could never be described as cultured but he gave everything, and would run through a brick wall for the team. He tackled hard and scored some vital goals, making him a popular player with the fans. 'Bish' thinks he's funny but his brother, John, is funnier and has made a successful living in stand-up comedy.

These were all players who had achieved little in their careers but when they were brought together on the training ground on the Wirral, a group of honest pros transformed into a great team and became cult figures with an ever-growing fan base.

We were like 'Kelly's Heroes' in the comedy/war film from the 1970s where a group of World War Two soldiers go AWOL to rob a bank behind enemy lines. Clint Eastwood, Donald Sutherland and company blow the bank doors off and head into the sunset after dividing the loot. Well, we were to do the business at many an away ground, and then head back up the M6 with the points!

Everybody understood each other's personalities and how they played. From where I was looking, I wanted people around me who knew how the game worked and what each plan of action was. We had a bit about us. We knew what people thought about us, and we were determined to show the difference between what they thought and what we could actually do. There is no doubt that the whole was bigger than the various parts.

It took a special man to create all that – and Johnny King was right up there with the best of them.

Chapter Twenty

THE GAFFER

'Now come on lads, we're going to war. Fix bayonets!

Johnny King was a phenomenal guy, quietly spoken but still capable of having a run-in with you. As I try to develop the coaching side of my game, I can appreciate even more what he went through in the job. He was a massive influence on me on and off the pitch.

The gaffer had played the game, making 264 appearances for Rovers in a playing career of over 400 games, so he knew football inside out. The Wembley years were part of his second spell as manager. Before that, he had already spent 14 years at the club as player, coach and manager.

He transferred this knowledge and experience and became the most successful manager in Tranmere's history. King got everyone talking about the club, and I often think back to how he achieved it. He built a succession of teams that were bold and who played with flair. A lot of emphasis was placed on quality wing play. The players got into the winning habit. When he plotted the successes he never gave anything away. He selected sides carefully and skilfully and was a very clever man-manager who would probably earn a mint these days using his people skills in business.

Mind you, he did come out with some strange stuff. King knew every player's strengths and weaknesses, and often compared his work to baking a cake: with him, the chef, and the players the ingredients that come together to make the final product! Johnny had a good line in phrases, well before Eric Cantona started spouting about seagulls and trawlers. I remember a post-match interview that he did on 'Match of the Day', so it must have been after an FA Cup match. King told a rather confused interviewer that "the squirrels have got the nuts out of the cupboard and now they are putting them back in!" How do you follow that? Some of his descriptions of individual players were brilliant. He used to say that Dave Martindale, with his silky skills, could "knit you a jumper with his feet!" As for Dave Higgins, well, Kingy nicknamed him 'the gas man' because he could smell danger!

We would be at the Valley Road training ground, and on a number of occasions Ronnie Moore or Kenny Jones's call would echo through the rabbit warren of corridors: "Send for Nico! The boss wants Nico in his office – now!" As I went in I would glance at the large portrait of Bill Shankly gazing down at me, and hear the gaffer's words: "Aah, the Nixon fella." He would try to inspire me to great achievements by referring to various Hollywood film stars:

"Man mountain, I need you to lead from the front. I want you to be like Kirk Douglas in Spartacus!"

He would often talk to us all about seeing a bird land on the bow of the ship:

"It's got a twig in its beak. You know what that means, don't you? It's near land. Go back and tell each player to grab an oar and row as hard as they can for the shore. I want people dancing on those oars as they row. If someone pulls an oar away someone else will go into the water. We have to row together."

As we got off the coach for away matches, it was always, "now come on lads, we're going to war. Fix bayonets!"

He seemed to have a phrase for everything. Signing players on loan was a bit like "trying to buy a sandwich from a garage. You can't be sure what you are going to get. Will it be mouldy cheese or prime Wiltshire ham?!"

The language was unusual but very effective. King described the club's rise through the divisions as a "rocket ride to the moon."

Tranmere's rise was like turning a jobbing professional boxer going nowhere in his career into a prize fighter – and people all over the country sat up and took notice. They were able to watch our Friday night action highlights on the Saturday lunchtime football programme, and see the quality of teams that we were beating along the way.

The increased exposure that Friday nights gave made us a lot of people's second favourite team.

When the gaffer celebrated the 20th anniversary of the day he started his second and spectacularly successful spell at Tranmere, the 'Liverpool Echo' asked me to select a team from the many players who had performed in front of me during the King years, as well as allowing me to add some comments.

The following team, which you'll see over the page, is set-up in a 4-4-2 formation...

Right-back: Steve Mungall (1979-1996) – 627 appearances, 17 goals.

'Steve's record speaks volumes and I can tell you he gave 100% in every game he played. He loved everything about the club. I don't think he got the recognition he deserved as a player. It would be nice to see former players like Mungy at the ground more often. He was able to do his job in a variety of positions. A great character.'

Centre-back: Dave Higgins (1983-1984, 1987-1997) – 434 appearances, 12 goals.

'He did a great job as a no-nonsense centre-half and was underestimated as a player in my opinion. He came into the club from non-League football and as the team progressed up the divisions, Higgy was able to raise his game up a notch, so he always looked accomplished no matter what level he was playing. He was also useful between the posts in an emergency a couple of times.'

Centre-back: Mark Hughes (1985-1994) – 344 appearances, 12 goals.

'Mark had a fantastic range of passing for a centre-back and a great ability for a big man – because he did have a tendency to put weight on. I liked to see him playing in front of me because he read the game so well.'

Left-back: Mark McCarrick (1987-1990) – 157 appearances, 16 goals.

Not one of the biggest names who played for Rovers but in the days when we were in the old Fourth and Third Divisions and making our way upwards, he was one of those who could be relied upon to give his all. Crackers McCarrick was strong and brave. I remember him scoring a winning goal for us once with his arm in a sling after he had dislocated it! That summed him up and showed the kind of spirit that we had in the squad at the time.'

Right midfield: Pat Nevin (1991-1992, 1992-1997) – 239 appearances, 39 goals.

'One of the top-quality international players who came into the club after we reached the old First Division. Players like Pat, Gary Stevens and John Aldridge had been playing at a higher level while we were doing all the hard work of climbing the divisions! Pat was an astute character who knew the game very well. He also knew how to put the ball on a pin and set up goals for the likes of John Aldridge.'

Centre midfield: Jim Harvey (1987-1992) – 239 appearances, 19 goals.

'Not a ball-winning midfielder, but someone who could produce something out of nothing for you. A silky passer who was very dangerous with free-kicks. I think that Jim's signing was proof that John King could really spot a player.'

Centre midfield: Dave Martindale (1987-1994) – 212 appearances, 12 goals.

'I think Dave was another who could have achieved more in the game. He was a great footballer in his own right. He came from Huyton, where a lot of good players have emerged over the years.

Dave had a reputation as a naughty boy but he could put the ball where he wanted on the football field.'

Left midfield: Johnny Morrissey (1985-1999) – 585 appearances, 64 goals.

'One of the best players I have ever worked with in the professional game. John was in the same mould as his father, who played for Everton, in that he was clever and creative, knew how to take a bit of stick and could give it out.'

Striker: Ian Muir (1985-1995) – 393 appearances, 180 goals.

'Tranmere's all-time leading scorer and a fine all-round player. Ian had the ability to make things happen. He could come off defenders, receive the ball, turn round and go at opponents – then feed the likes of Johnny Morrissey and get into the box for the cross.'

Striker: John Aldridge (1991-1998) – 294 appearances, 174 goals.

'Inside the penalty area, Aldo was a natural who could finish from anywhere if people made chances for him. He benefited from brilliant service from the likes of John Morrissey and Pat Nevin – and he made the most of it.'

There were some difficult choices to make, but the comments about the ones that I did pick said a lot about the type of players that we had at the club. Johnny King rated Aldo so highly that he compared him to 'El Cid': "Even when he's dead you could strap him to a trolley, wheel him to the far post and he'd still knock one in!" Johnny got to the stage where everyone at the club believed that anything was possible under him. He remained involved until 2003 and I will remember him as the best manager in Tranmere's history. Kingy was a true legend.

Chapter Twenty One

ALL SHOOK UP

'I remember thinking this is what it must be like when you die...'

For a brief period in October 2001, I even kept my playing career going. I went to Kidderminster Harriers on loan where my mate, Jan Molby, was manager. The former Liverpool legend had a goalkeeper who was suspended so I helped him out. I was a bit of 'polyfilla' for him, but managed to keep clean sheets in the three games that I played for the club, who were still in the Football League. In the space of a week I fitted in league matches at home to Cheltenham Town and away at Carlisle United as well as an LDV Vans Trophy game at Doncaster Rovers. I got a few bob in the arse pocket and was glad to help out. I still see a lot of Jan, and his wife, Mandy, to this day. They are active in charity work on Merseyside and are good friends of Rachel and myself.

I had been goalkeeping coach for about three seasons when

Tranmere awarded me a testimonial season in 2002/03. My testimonial match was against Manchester City on 6th August 2002 and it was a great night with loads of former players, celebrities and current players involved as well as, of course, my family. It started with a Celebrity Match between Johnny King's Legends and Kevin Keegan's All Stars, which I took part in. Funnily enough, the opposing keeper was Andy Dibble, whose arrival at Maine Road had led to my departure and a life on the Wirral.

The main event was the Tranmere Rovers v Manchester City match. I compiled a Dream Team for the programme, made up of a selection of the many professionals that I had played alongside throughout my career. It read:

Danny Coyne

Mark Hughes ***Steve Vickers***

Dave Higgins ***Mark McCarrick***

Neil McNab ***Dave Martindale***

Johnny Morrissey ***Paul Cook***

Ian Muir ***John Aldridge***

I wrote little pen portraits for each of the players. Danny Coyne's read:

'This was an easy choice for me because I couldn't pick myself. Danny is not the biggest or tallest goalkeeper but he compensated for that by being brave as a lion, very good technically and possessing the ability to make saves from seemingly impossible positions. He also had the added benefit of being coached by yours truly.'

As for defender Mark Hughes:

'The original Tranmere sweeper, he had the ability to land

a ball on a sixpence. He could read the game really well and was a clever footballer. He is also my best mate so I had to pick him.'

And John Aldridge's read:

'A unique talent. Could score goals for fun. A legend at the club, he was so good he is up there alongside me!'

Comedian, Stan Boardman, poked fun at me:

'Eric was a Caesarian birth which does not affect him except when he gets out of his car – he always climbs out of the sun roof. He went to a really tough school. Katie Adie was the teacher and they had broken leg of lamb for dinners. When Eric was signed from City the Tranmere board spared no expense and sent a bike for him. When he arrived two days later he signed immediately and was given £50 and a hamper. Johnny King once compared Eric to Gordon Banks – he said: "Compared to Banksie you're crap!"'

My managerial hero, Johnny King, also wrote a lovely piece about my contribution to the club:

'Eric was one of the first pieces in the jigsaw when building my team. Goalkeepers are one of the more eccentric beings in football and Eric was certainly one of those. I think you have to be a little mad to be a goalkeeper! Eric had a great pair of hands and like Bill Shankly I tried to build a good spine in the team from keeper and centre-half through to centre-forward.

Eric was always a tremendous competitor and could shout well to get his fellow defenders motivated. He became a wonderful servant for Tranmere Rovers Football Club and I am very proud of the fact that he was able to be around to see some great and wonderful occasions at the club. For me, Eric epitomises the true professional footballer and he deserves this night of celebration.

Good luck to him and his family on this special night. It was a pleasure to work with him.'

It was a very emotional evening at Prenton Park and I will always be grateful to Kevin Keegan for bringing his side and the fantastic City fans, allowing me to join together the two parts of my professional career.

Throughout my career I had dived around like a madman and put my body through absolute purgatory in the gym. Rheumatism was beginning to affect me and, one day, the knees finally gave up.

It was 2003 and I'd had enough of limping to training and having to stand up straight for 10 seconds after getting out of the car. Tranmere had given me insurance cover so I decided to get my right knee done as it was in so much pain. Quality of life was important to me and I could never understand why some people were unwilling to have operations to improve joints like knees and hips.

Rob Harvey performed the operation at Murrayfield Hospital on the Wirral, about 10 minutes from home. Rob is a fantastic surgeon who I still bump into from time to time at Manchester City matches. Tranmere physio, Les Parry, asked if he could come into the operating theatre with his camera. He was being serious! He had never seen a knee operation before and wanted some pictures. It takes all sorts! It was a good job we were close mates.

Recovery seemed to be going well, but things took a sharp turn for the worse. The knee became infected. I was on morphine, and still feeling too much pain for my own good. The physio would come in and bend the leg. I kept telling her it wasn't right but she thought I was being a bit of a baby. I always thought that I had a high pain threshold but this was something else. Before long, my knee then swelled up to the size of a rugby ball. Rob looked at it and took me straight to surgery. I was still in my own bed with my boxer shorts on. There had been no time to get prepared.

I went into shock and honestly thought that it was the end of me. I had never experienced so much pain, and felt like I was drifting away. I remember thinking that this is what it must be like when you die. Everything seemed to be shutting down and no one seemed to be listening anything I was saying. I remember thinking that my hands seemed transparent, and that I could see right through them.

Images of Rachel and my kids came into my mind. Rachel, meanwhile, had been contacted early in the morning by one of her client's in her hairdressing business. The lady was a sister at the hospital and told her that things had deteriorated. I was quite poorly and the staff couldn't get to the bottom of the problem. Rachel immediately made arrangements to get the kids to school and young Bradley to her mother's. By the time she arrived I had gone down to surgery.

The medical staff re-opened my knee and removed 12 pounds of material caused by the infection. I woke up and before I knew it things were improving. I had lost three stone and, looking back, it is hard to find words to describe the experience I had been through. Certainly it was far worse than the heart attack because I had felt under control before. I knew where I was and why I was in there. This experience was something altogether more frightening.

Rob told Rachel that I'd been very ill and needed lots of rest. She visited me three times a day, fitting me in around hair appointments and her responsibilities to the children. She tried to get me to eat a varied diet, but all I wanted was fruit. She nursed me well, so much so that, later that year, we got married in Las Vegas! My best men were two old mates, Keith Nethercott and Eamonn Kenny.

Six of us went out and we had a great time. I was soon back to my mischievous best. We were at the MGM Grand, which was the largest hotel in the world when it opened in 1993.

It's an amazing place on the Strip in Vegas and in amongst all the facilities I found a joke shop. I love playing tricks on people and finding this place gave me loads of amusement, much to the dismay of my mates..

I bought stink bombs, invisible ink and cans of horrible oil, one of which went over Keith while he was sunbathing, and a machine that gave an electric shock. You would hold it in the palm of your hand and it was attached by a wire to a charger, which was triggered when someone shook your hand and pressed the button. Hours of fun followed round the pool on my stag night as I went round shaking hands here, there and everywhere and watching the reactions from the unsuspecting public. Keith, the dutiful best man, insisted that I left the device behind in my room on the day of the wedding. Enough was enough and we had all enjoyed a laugh.

The ceremony was streamed live on the internet and people all around the world saw me and Keith walking down the aisle to meet the vicar before the service.

I shook hands with him and everyone watching at home was in stitches, texting us asking, 'What happened then? Why did the vicar suddenly shake?'!

Rachel's sister saw it on a cruise ship in the Mediterranean, her aunty was in Canada and I had some mates tuning in from Gran Canaria! The only down side to the whole experience was that I couldn't wear my Elvis suit, but it was a small price to pay in order to marry the girl that I loved.

Rachel and I have known each other for around 20 years. Before that time, she tells a story about going out to a club with friends when one of them said: "There's Eric Nixon!"

Rachel replied: "Who's Eric Nixon? The friend replied that he was the Tranmere goalkeeper.

Rachel, apparently, went along the bar to ask for my autograph. When I agreed to sign, she said: "On my arse!" and she just walked off!

We were originally part of a bigger crowd who came together for events like her 30th birthday party, which was held at my house, and she and her husband would go on holiday with me and my wife. I remember that Rachel and I were the two out of the four who had a laugh together. Eventually, her partner went off to the Isle of Man and I left Tranmere – and my second wife – for Stockport.

I used to take the children round to Rachel's house as it was good to have someone to talk to at a difficult time, and Rachel had known Karen well – in fact, she was godmother to my daughter, Jessica!

On one occasion when I pitched up, Rachel clearly felt that there was nothing to say and hid behind the door! I guess she was getting over her own problems and didn't want another barrow load of mine.

Everyone, including my daughter, thought we were having an affair, but we were not. In fact, I did not fancy her one bit. I did ask her out for a drink on one occasion and she said, "Why? I don't fancy you." I told her the same, but that I just thought she might want to get out from within her four walls. About two weeks later, she was still staring at the walls so she took me up on my offer.

After we started our relationship, Steve, Rachel's ex, told her how surprised he was because she had often told him that she did not fancy me. We soon grew closer and she is very special to me. She makes me laugh, understands me and is always there for me.

We share our lives with our son, Bradley, who was born in 2002, and Eric Junior, Jessica and Amy from previous relationships. Rachel is my best mate and I love her to bits. Among her many friends across the Wirral are the daughters of my old boss, Johnny King.

She was within a group at Chester Races one day when she suddenly heard a voice shouting "Rachel, Rachel!"

It was John Aldridge, who she knows well. Rachel acknowledged the greeting and carried on talking to her disbelieving colleagues, who could not understand why she did not go across and talk to the great man. Rachel's answer was that he could wait for her!

Chapter Twenty Two

LIFE AFTER FOOTBALL

'You cannot change the sands of time but you can still do something about it'

John Aldridge had finally left Tranmere in March 2000, to be replaced briefly by caretakers Kevin Sheedy and Ray Mathias. During his five years in charge, Aldo had kept the club in Division One despite financial difficulties. He cleverly blended free transfers with bright young talent, and there were some giant-killing cup wins which helped to keep the club's name in the national newspapers.

One young player with a special talent was Dave Challinor, who became a good mate of mine. Dave was a typical centre-half, gangly and tall, and had been playing in the West Cheshire League for Bromborough Pool. Dave had to wait his chance for first-team football, but Aldo had noticed how far he could throw a football. He worked with his coaching staff to turn this into a weapon in the team's armoury. Dave was amazing, and able to land the ball in the goal from the halfway line without it bouncing! In matches he was well capable of finding the far side of the penalty area from the touchline and not only with a looping throw but with a low, fast missile. Teams became very reluctant to concede anything in our attacking third, and even tried to physically stop Dave from using his throw!

On one occasion, I was substitute and sitting alongside Aldo on the bench. Everytime Dave got the ball to launch one of his specials from the touchline, the opposition would get one of their subs to stand in his way, knowing that he couldn't throw from behind the advertising hoardings! This was beginning to piss Aldo off and he told me to sort it. I ran up the touchline, rugby-tackled the sub, Dave got his throw-in and we scored!

Dave was phenomenal. They talk about Stoke's Rory Delap today but he was nowhere compared to our man. We set up a publicity stunt on the seafront at New Brighton Dips, and lined cars up bonnet to bumper. I think he cleared about 15!

He also took part in a special challenge set up at Prenton Park in about 1998 where he went into the 'Guinness Book of Records' with a throw of over 46 metres, beating the previous record held by Andy Legg, the former Welsh international.

An amateur player from Yorkshire has since beaten it, but Dave's remains the longest throw-in in the professional game, and it was an extra weapon that no team liked to face.

Another thing that John Aldridge the manager had realised was that to match the threat from richer clubs in the league it was necessary to put opponents off their stride, and make Prenton Park a difficult place to come to. It worked, by and large, but Aldo eventually resigned after writing his chapter in the Tranmere history, both as a player and as a manager. He is a fantastic person, a great mate and Tranmere did one of the best bits of business ever when they took him from Spain. We tried to talk him out of leaving but he had had his fill and, suddenly, enough was enough for this emotional character. One day, after a home defeat by Barnsley, he told me: "I've had enough, Nico." He went upstairs, resigned and walked away.

The team had been relegated by the end of the season, and the new campaign began with Dave Watson in charge. The ex-Everton and England defender had just ended his playing career at the age of 39, and moved across the Mersey with the specific aim of getting Rovers back into the First Division.

His arrival at the club did not meet with everyone's approval, and several club favourites were overlooked for the position. With the cards stacked against him, Watson found it difficult to make progress and was sacked after one season in charge. In fact, he was to leave on 1st August, just five days before my testimonial game, having contributed a piece for the programme! There haven't been many occasions when a manager has gone after performances in pre-season matches, but the statement that came out from the club referred to a 'lack of passion and pride by the players'.

'Waggy' was a smashing guy and extremely nice. He always treated his staff well, but also brought in a lot of new approaches which were not to my liking at the time. Under him, we heard more about the importance of diet and fitness drinks and a different type of fitness regime. Previously, diet had centred around booze! There was also a guy who started to take over training – again, a really nice fella, but he got in Les Parry's way. Unfortunately, Dave Watson never had the respect as a manager that he had as a player.

Ray Mathias, his number two, was finally installed as manager, rather than caretaker, for the 2002/03 season. A lot of fans were delighted with the appointment because Ray had given the club some outstanding service over a long time. He had done virtually every job going at Tranmere over 30-odd years and played over 600 games. It wasn't the best of starts for Ray, though, when the Jason Koumas transfer deprived him of a star player after a few weeks.

Eventually, he went the same way as Watson just after the start of the following season, despite the side finishing seventh under him in 2002/03. A home defeat to Wrexham was the final straw for a board who didn't wait long after the game before making the decision. It wasn't popular with the fans, but that's the way it is in this results business.

Tranmere turned briefly to youth-team coach, John McMahon, as caretaker before Brian Little took over in October 2003. I knew Brian well from my days at Wolves and he was a good man. He concentrated on sorting the defence out first before adopting a more attacking style, and the team ended up finishing a respectable eighth.

A few months earlier, I had met up with Colin West, who had helped Chris Turner guide Hartlepool United to three successive play-offs. The pair were now at Sheffield Wednesday and were good mates of mine, and asked me if I would go to Hillsborough to do some coaching.

I joined in July 2003 and started working with Kevin Pressman and the other keepers. I also had another arrangement with Tranmere which left me doing three days a week in Yorkshire and two on the Wirral, criss-crossing the Pennines on my high-powered motorbike! I spent a season with Wednesday and became their oldest player. I had been Tranmere's oldest player and now I was Sheffield Wednesday's! Kevin Pressman went off just before the half-hour mark and I was eligible to take his place after being registered following an injury to Ola Tidman. As my old mate, Steve Mungall, would say: "They must have taken Nico on in instalments!"

Chris and Colin got the sack in September 2004 and my time at Hillsborough was over. Brian Little called me in and asked if I wanted to help the goalkeepers every day. No problem! Tranmere was my priority, but the opportunity also gave me more time to devote to business ventures that I was looking to invest in on the Wirral, following my decision to finally hang up my gloves after Wednesday's match against Grimsby.

My job at Rovers was to put pressure on the consistent and dedicated number one, John Achterberg, by bringing the best out of current number two, Russell Howarth, and teenage prospect, Phil Palethorpe. It was no good being a Mr Nice Guy, a number two happy to accept second best. I was far from that as a player. You have got to aim to be number one otherwise there's no point in being a professional footballer. It's dog eat dog in football, as it is in life, and I worked hard to try and get that driven into Russell and Phil.

Away from the ground I dabbled in a few businesses as I attempted to build a new life outside football. Having been employed by the likes of John Flemings and Auto Cleanse before I played professionally, the workplace beckoned again. I had rented a garage just down the road from Prenton Park and returned to former days by turning it into the Blue Monkey Hand Car Wash! A strange name, I'm sure you'll agree, and it came about because Eric Junior had a blue monkey hanging on the end of his bed. I just thought that it was the sort of name that would get people talking. Through the business I was able to give a few young local lads a chance of a bit of work.

I went into business with Derek 'Potter' Johnson, and I also had a part-share in a cafe. I drove an old silver V8 Jaguar looking a bit like Arthur Daley in 'Minder', the comedy-drama about London's criminal underworld. I loved that car!

After 18 months or so, I decided to give up the coaching work for Brian, and set my sights on gaining a fitness qualification. I had always shown a strong commitment to fitness, shaped by my two near-death experiences in hospital, and enjoyed keeping fit. I had rarely missed a day's training as a player. I also knew my limitations and was aware that I was past my prime and putting weight on, but still wanted to be able to do the simple things like playing football in the garden with Bradley. I also wanted the chance to educate people about issues such as diabetes and obesity. You cannot change the sands of time, but you can still do something about it.

Leaving the football club was a difficult decision to make, but my dream was to run a successful health and fitness business that people would understand. My place was to be the real deal, a personalised gym where I provided a programme and acted on it. No two people are the same. It's not just about pumping heavy weights and how fast you can run. The ideas were all there in my head, and the fitness qualification had been a massive help. I knew exactly what I wanted to achieve and did for a while but, in the end, it just did not work out.

A lot of people would come to Tranmere matches every fortnight or so and see the gym, but wouldn't take it further. I found myself clicking my heels waiting for custom and, unfortunately, I was not skilled enough in marketing to be able to get the message out. I decided to cut my losses. A guy came in and made me an offer for the equipment. I told him he could have it if he got it out the next day. He did just that, and that was it – I shut the gym down.

Chapter Twenty Three

LOVE ME TENDER

'Cancer – the very word fills you with dread'

There was light at the end of the tunnel after the disappointment of the gym. My best man and good friend, Keith Nethercott, offered me the chance to join him in Dubai.

Keith loves his football and is a big Liverpool supporter. He was developing his glass business in Dubai and threw me a lifeline. I went over to stay with him in the Arabian Ranches residential area, where he was living alone in a five-bedroomed property. Keith loaned me some money to get me going. He put a word in at the local golf club, telling them that an ex-professional footballer was coming over and starting up as a personal trainer. Twelve signed up immediately.

Things started well and I enjoyed the social side, particularly Saturday afternoons, when everyone would go out for an afternoon drink. We often went to one of the pubs owned by the Sheikh and I would do my Elvis routine for them! When

I went over, it was the final day of the Dubai Desert Classic, one of the richest golf tournaments in the world. All the top players were there, many attracted by large appearance fees. I arrived in town, dropped my bags off and headed for the golf club. Within 20 minutes of arriving I find myself entertaining Tiger Woods and all with some Elvis songs!

I intended to start a business in the Middle East, but it turned out to be harder than I thought. There were all sorts of issues to come to terms with, and red tape up to your knees. There was a clientele to be built up, tax and visa issues and you had to pay up to £20,000 just to be able to work.

With the intense heat, I had to be up at 5am and finish at 2pm. I stuck at it for eight to 10 months. I had left my family back in England and, as time moved on, it was becoming harder rather than easier to get clients. The clinching factor in the end was that Rachel, who had been brilliant about me going in the first place, was learning to live without me. I remember it was a Saturday when that truth dawned on me and I was on a flight back to England on the Monday morning. I had at least repaid Keith's loan and made a bit for myself.

I made use of my fitness qualification and set up a base at the large JJB multi-gym complex at Bromborough. They are good gyms and very popular. However, I was stumping up £500 per month on rent, which was soul-destroying. They had their own rules and regulations, what you could and could not do. What annoyed me was the number of fitness instructors who seemed to know the language, but not what it all meant. They didn't properly understand how the body worked and they seemed to be there just to 'talk the talk'. In the end, the politics got too much for me and I called it a day after about six months.

During this period I was drawn back to football again. I became goalkeeping coach at Fleetwood Town, a non-League side on the Lancashire coast. It was funny how it came about. Having tried to get a few businesses off the ground over the previous two years or so, things had not gone as smoothly as I had hoped. I was thinking about a return to day-to-day involvement at a professional club. I believed that my experience and knowledge, my coaching qualifications and my fitness background could be put to good use. With this in mind, I had applied for the manager's job at non-League Hyde United in Manchester. I had worked under some good managers and learned from them all. I was putting my hand up and letting people know that I was serious about getting back into the game. I wanted to pit my wits against other managers and teams and see how I could progress with a group of lads whose approach had my personality stamped on them. There were others like me, eager to make a start and with fresh ideas, but clubs were too often going back to the same old names.

I honestly felt that I was good enough to manage a league club, but Hyde would be an attractive challenge not too far from my home base. They played in the Blue Square North, one level down from the Conference. Anyway, I rang my old Blackpool and Tranmere mate, Micky Mellon, to see if he fancied coming along as my assistant. He told me that he had just got the manager's job at Fleetwood Town, and offered me the chance to join him as goalkeeping coach. It was very tempting. I gave it a lot of thought, and weighed the alternatives up. Here was a new challenge, working with a guy who I had always respected as a player and who was one of my best mates. Fleetwood was an ambitious club who were putting their name on the non-League map in the North West.

The Hyde job, on the other hand, would allow me to get

back in the game as a manager with overall responsibility. It would be exciting but the buck would stop with me, and was I ready for the stresses that it would undoubtedly bring? Plus, I hadn't even been offered an interview yet!

In the end, I went with Micky. Fleetwood Town were also in the Blue Square North, having risen dramatically up the non-League structure. Their ambitious chairman, Andy Pilley, was investing heavily in the club but, when Micky and I joined, they were down near the bottom of the table. Respectability was reached over the rest of the season and, in 2009/10, the club gained promotion to the Conference through the play-offs. They had been denied automatic promotion as champions having controversially lost points when Farsley Celtic went out of operation, and clubs were then made to forfeit the points that they had gained in matches against the Yorkshire club. However, all was well in the end, and Fleetwood got past Droylsden and Alfreton to bring the chairman's dream of league football one step closer. Excitement mounted as Town then made their mark at the top level and a second successive play-off position was achieved, with the club losing out to eventual play-off winners AFC Wimbledon.

I enjoyed the job immensely and, the family of football being as it is, it was not long before I met up with familiar faces on the non-League circuit. Brian Little was managing Gainsborough Trinity while my old mate at Prenton Park, Jim Harvey, had become boss at Stalybridge Celtic in 2010, after achieving great success at Morecambe.

Andy Pilley was a chairman who loved his football and he had assembled a strong squad. It contained a nucleus of players who knew the non-League scene, and some former League professionals who added their experience of playing at the top of the football pyramid. Full-back Alan Wright had enjoyed a stellar career with Blackburn Rovers, Aston Villa and others, and had the claim to fame of being the shortest player to play in the Premier League. What he lacked in height he made up for in stature, and was still a class act who rarely put a foot wrong. John Hills, also a full-back, had been at Everton before returning to his hometown club Blackpool where he made 157 appearances in a league career totalling nearly 300 games. Midfielder Jamie Milligan had also been at Everton and played for Blackpool while defender Sean Gregan had been to the top with the likes of Leeds United and West Bromwich Albion.

Experience could also be found in spadefuls in the backroom staff. There was Micky himself, of course, with nearly 500 games under his belt at Bristol City, West Bromwich Albion and Burnley along with, of course, Blackpool and Tranmere.

Alongside him was another face from the past, Steve Macauley. Steve's a great guy and was one of the talented young apprentices at Manchester City when I arrived. He and Mark Seagraves often played together in central defence in front of me at Maine Road and I rated him highly, although I probably scared him into not making a mistake as he and Mark felt the full force of my voice on many an occasion! Steve played most of his games, just over 300, at Crewe Alexandra in a 10-year period from 1992 before leaving the game to train as a physiotherapist, which he still practises. Steve was always an honest lad and I think that this made me warm to him. We're still good mates and I respect him highly as a coach.

While I was at Fleetwood, I also met up again with Craig Madden, who had played for Bury all those years ago in the League Cup when I made that save from Trevor Ross, one of my finest. Craig, another former Blackpool player, had come from Stockport County to be Micky's assistant-manager.

Another good mate of mine, Ian Liversedge, had been recruited as physio. 'SOS', as he is known throughout the game, had gathered nearly 30 years of experience which had started, strangely enough, back at Tranmere. The club physio had sadly died on the beach during a training session. 'SOS' was in his final year at university and offered to help out as they had a run of injuries and the busy Christmas period ahead. They agreed to pay him £5 per week and kick-started a career which took him to Newcastle United, Oldham Athletic alongside Joe Royle, and to the Northern Ireland set-up. In 2010 I entertained the guests at his wedding with my Elvis show!

I was surrounded by experienced people who enjoyed a good laugh and it made for an enjoyable place to work. I did a good job with the coaching, to be fair, and the standard of goalkeeping at the club improved with all the guys I worked with performing well for the first team at one stage or another.

Danny Hurst had come up through the leagues with Fleetwood and was a great favourite of the fans. He is now at Conference side, Barrow. Scott Davies was signed from Morecambe having played for the Shrimps in a play-off at Wembley while Craig Dootson was a larger-than-life character, not unlike myself. Craig had already endeared himself to the Cod Army before he arrived in Fleetwood, taking them on with plenty of banter in the opposition goal for clubs like Hyde United. He cemented that status before moving on to Altrincham in the Conference and Kendal Town.

I left briefly at the end of the promotion year but returned just after the start of the club's first season in the Conference. I had gone down to watch a game and spoke to Micky, who asked what I was doing and suggested that I came back.

Scott Davies had arrived from Morecambe by the time I returned to Fleetwood. He was my first challenge. Scott had all the attributes. He was fit, ambitious and agile but, he could also be erratic. He would run around at a hundred miles an hour, making mistakes and not appreciating how the game should be played. I sat him down and talked about a young keeper with the same attitude in the 1980s – me. I had learnt from the experience and here in front of me was a young, talented professional who could do the same and go on to great things in the future.

I told Scott that he shouldn't rush into situations that you cannot get out of. I made it clear that you don't worry about the ball once it has crossed beyond the halfway line. I told him to concentrate on looking after his back four, his back three, and to make sure his wingers were tucked in. He needed to think all the time and make the game work for him. We talked about keeping concentration levels up when play was at the other end of the pitch.

Scotty was in direct competition with Danny Hurst. Danny was a quite different type of guy. He was a club legend, keeping forwards at bay for years and gaining cult status with a dramatic penalty save in a play-off shoot-out against Droylsden in 2010. Danny was a more laid-back character, too much so at times when he needed a rocket up his arse. He was older and more experienced than Scott, and it all made for an interesting challenge as I tried to keep both of them happy.

I enjoyed working with both lads. I was always direct and honest but supported them through the highs and lows that made up the tale of the first Conference season in 2010/11. Danny started with the shirt, came out for a cross at Crawley Town in the opening minutes of the game at the start of September, and a heavy fall on his shoulder put him out for months. The lad was understandably devastated after showing good form until that point. On came Scott for his debut, straight into the path of a rampant Crawley, who were to become champions. The siege ended, Town came back to gain a brilliant draw and Scott's Fleetwood career was up and running. He went on a run of excellent form, whilst all the time supporting Danny's recovery. He kept his colleague at bay when fitness returned but the odd error crept in, and Danny got the shirt back. I then had to turn my attention to Scott and help him cope with the disappointment of rejection. He dealt with it brilliantly and came back a stronger keeper. I'm biased, I know but I didn't see any better keepers in the league than our two and they each learned so much from coping with setbacks.

By the end of the season, it became apparent from behind the scenes as contracts were being discussed and finances considered that one of my two star keepers might have to leave. I let my feelings be known. It did not seem right to me when strikers in the squad were ten-a-penny that the club risked leaving themselves vulnerable at the back. When Danny's contract was ended I felt for him, and it took me back all those years to Maine Road when Andy Dibble came to the club, a move that led to me leaving Manchester City. Fleetwood had clearly put their faith in Scott Davies as the face of the future. I could see where they were coming from as he is a fine prospect who I rate highly enough to think that, one day, he will play in the Football League, hopefully for Fleetwood.

To Danny's credit, he dusted himself down and signed for fellow-Conference side, Barrow, where he quickly made an impact. It took a lot of character and balls to do that, and I admire Danny for doing it.

I was a proud man in August 2011 when both Danny and Scott saved penalties on the same day. This was one area where I gave them the benefit of my experience gained from a career of facing up to the ball on that spot 12 yards away. This can be a nerve-wracking time for a keeper, particularly if you are in front of the opposition's screaming fans. As with other parts of my game, I developed a technique and learnt from every kick that I faced. I used to let the striker see me going one way then I would dive the other. I found that it worked more often than not.

Both penalty saves were in games that ended in 1-0 victories, Fleetwood Town at home to Hayes & Yeading and Barrow at Bath City. This underlined the importance even more of the goalkeepers' work. A few days later, I travelled from the Wirral to Barrow to see the two guys in action against each other, a match which Danny will have remembered more fondly than Scott! I watched the game from the stands as, by then, I had left Fleetwood Town for the second, and final time. The decision to let one of the two class acts go in the summer had not rested easily with me but it had definitely been an enjoyable period. I had a good relationship with the fans and the staff, and it was brilliant to watch the improvements off the pitch as well as on it. I still watch their matches when I am available.

I also learnt a lot about management from Micky Mellon. I liked his calm, collected way of doing things, and it gave me the belief that I could be a manager myself one day. My old mate trusted me to get on with my job and appreciated the way in which his goalkeepers improved under my guidance.

As Fleetwood was a part-time job, I had the opportunity to look at other options such as the 'Eric Nixon Pro Stoppers UK', which was a goalkeeping clinic that I launched in Birkenhead. It was designed to improve the skills of young boys and girls between the ages of eight and 16. There isn't enough specialist advice and coaching for goalkeepers, and I was trying to redress the balance. You'll find coaches and scouts all over the land out on a Sunday morning looking for athletic young strikers who can bang the ball in, but keepers don't seem to be in demand as much.

It was dawning on me loud and clear that life after football was not a bed of roses. I had been busy trying different things but, for one reason or another, seemed incapable of seeing them through and finding that one opportunity that would secure my future. I often felt that I was drifting along and it was beginning to get to me. There had been difficult times as a player when you doubted yourself and confidence dipped, but I had always lifted myself and come out at the other side stronger and wiser. There would inevitably be someone alongside you to put an arm around your shoulder. Now there was no arm available.

You knew where you were as a footballer. The game had carried me for over 20 years. As long as you trained hard and stayed injury free, everything was mapped out and organised for you from pre-season training to the summer holidays with the lads in Magaluf. You were given the time to be at the airport, the ground, the team coach and the training ground, and all you had to do was make sure you were there. Your kit was laid out for you, your boots were cleaned and you were even told where and what to autograph for fans.

There was no one there to do that for me now, and no one around me to share the experience. I had gone from the heart of a team ethic to become an individual with bills to pay. For someone as outgoing and extrovert as me that was particularly hard to come to terms with.

I'm sure that I'm not alone in feeling this way. This is a realisation that must hit many a former professional. You've packed your kit up for the last time and left the ground. Monday morning dawns, you have kicked your last ball, pointed your finger accusingly at your last opponent and made your last joke. The dressing room spirit and camaraderie was continuing but you were no longer part of it. Former team-mates with their nicknames and their practical jokes were moving on and leaving you behind at the side of the road, alone. Ahead lies a very long highway – 30 or 40 empty years which needed to be filled and they are taunting you, 'Now what are you going to do with yourself?'

I never had an agent to fight my corner. Managers and chairmen wouldn't tolerate them in those days. They were more intimidating with a 'shut up and get on with it' philosophy. I had taken a modest lump sum but there was no financial advice from Tranmere. The players didn't think of investing. You got what you could, when you could, and you tried to play as often as you could – and then got on with the rest of your life.

I got some help from the Professional Footballers' Association, particularly Oshor Williams, but could have had more. It's a real culture shock and clubs and the PFA need to look at this more. The 18 and 19-year-olds are taught about writing a CV when it's the played aged 30 and over who need that help. Despite all those years in the game, I had no CV experience when I most needed it.

Joining the queues at the Job Centre or Job Seekers wasn't easy because, for a start, you have no idea what you want to do and, secondly, you get all the locals looking at you and thinking, 'you shouldn't be here.' Well, get real, because we are.

You have to believe that Eric Nixon is going to be there, so are many others. We have all got mouths to feed.

The Fleetwood Town experience had showed how much I had missed what makes up the day-to-day life of a footballer. The nearest fix still available was the Masters series, which has become so popular through Sky Sports' coverage. It's a six-a-side competition for over-35s and has allowed me to team up with old mates from Tranmere, Manchester City and Wolves, as well as being a great opportunity to let the banter fly in the dressing room. Tranmere have had a great record in the competition, winning the Merseyside Masters three years running and the Grand Final itself in 2009. I joined the lads for the 2011 event at the Liverpool Echo Arena. We lost to Wigan and Bolton, but it did not stop the chat and the laughs with the likes of Brannan, Irons and Bishop. It was also good to see so many supporters making the short journey through the tunnel. When I played for Wolves I was alongside Steve Bull, Andy Thompson, Paul Cook and Don Goodman. We had a good run before losing to Liverpool. It was brilliant while it lasted, but not something that you can build a new career round.

If I had taken the view that the world owed me a living because I'd played football and hadn't left the house until it happened, then I would have had no excuses. But it's just not been like that. What really irritates me is that I have got off my backside and devoted a lot of time and money to strengthen my chances of a permanent job. While I've been dipping in and out of the various jobs that I've already described, I've spent much of my 'spare time' over the last 10 years putting in some hard graft at college. I've had to plan lessons around my other commitments and travel hundreds and hundreds of miles, spending thousands of pounds in the process, around the North-West. I've regularly sat up until four in the morning doing essays with my wife wondering what I'm up to but the job's done and I'm proud of what I've achieved because I was never an academic worker at school.

I've driven myself on and gained an impressive list of qualifications. As well as the Advanced Level Three fitness qualification with which I set up the gym, I have a UEFA goalkeeping coaching and football coach 'A' licence and I am an A1 Assessor, which qualifies me to assess, tutor and coach students in schools and colleges doing NVQs and BTECs around sport and recreation. There are many others besides.

I've reached the stage where I want to use these qualifications to get an opportunity to go and show people what I can do, to nail down a role which will make me as successful off the pitch as I was on it. I want someone to open their mind up and see that. I don't deserve the chance because I'm an ex-footballer, but I do because I've gone and got myself qualified. The trouble is that when people look at Eric Nixon they see a goalkeeper who sings Elvis songs and nothing else. They do not see the other strings that I've got to my bow. They don't see the health and fitness expert and the nutritional adviser. I have a passion for fitness and sport and do not want to be pigeonholed as a guy who can do nothing but coach goalkeepers.

It's time I started exploiting the graft I've put in over the last 10 years, and one thing I've done is to approach schools and colleges to look for opportunities. I decided I would be better-placed on the inside looking out, rather than the other way round, and I've had positive reactions. If you get out and show people the commitment that you have for the job you want to do, then that speaks volumes about you as a person.

I know I won't become a teacher as I'll need a degree, but I think that I have more than enough qualifications to become an assistant. This would give me a chance to get my messages across about subjects that I feel passionately about, and get the word into the primary schools about healthy living in such a way that the kids are inspired to pass it on to mums and dads.

In the end it's all down to the kids and young people, getting them to have a passion for sport and a positive attitude to healthy living which will keep them off the streets. I have a lifetime's experience to give to them as well as the education gained from the many courses that I've been on. That is experience that cannot be ignored.

I owe it to Rachel and the kids to provide for them, and that's what constantly drives me on. Others have had an opportunity to build a life for themselves after football. I haven't. If I had a steady job year in, year out, with a pension waiting for me at the age of 65 I'd be happy; but it's just not happened. I've chased the full-time appointment and it seems to have gone on forever. Some think that I just flit from one thing to the next and back again but it's not like that. I'm a trustworthy and loyal guy who just cannot nail down the step that will take me through to retirement.

While I have been trying to gain regular employment, my good friend Keith Nethercott has been a big help and I have been doing some work as a salesman for his glass company. This takes me all over the place and Keith is looking to expand it to Dubai so you never know, I could be back out in the heat one day! Keith must think that my gift of the gab will help! The company is called GlassRoom Extensions and the job is only part-time at the moment, but it is introducing me to a whole new world and showing me how business works.

If I'd played in the modern era it would have been much different. One contract in the Premier League would have set me and my generation up for life. There are players not a million miles from me who are earning upwards of £50,000 a week just to sit in the stands at the Etihad Stadium. They will end up taking more out of football than they put in whereas, with me, it's the other way round. Just think what I'd be on now if I was signing for my beloved Manchester City today. Saying that, I don't begrudge the modern player cashing in because, let's face it, we'd all take it. I do think, though, that we've reached the point where it needs to have a cap put on it all. Anyway, as I keep telling myself, 'don't look back in anger'!

As I have adjusted to life beyond football, Rachel has been my rock and constant support and I love her so much. I wouldn't even swap her for a new pair of goalkeeping gloves! It has not always been easy for her as I have flitted from one type of work to another and, having been through a life-threatening experience in hospital with me, she was to endure her own heartache and go through a time when I had to be strong for her.

I've been a patron of Claire House on the Wirral for 20 years. It is a children's hospice based at Bebington and I have met many brave boys and girls suffering in many ways. I have also had the pleasure and privilege to be able to raise money for the cause. One such example was organising a six-a-side football competition for a little girl, Ruby Atwell, who was 15 months old at the time and suffering from throat cancer. Never for one moment did I think that the kind of illness that I observed in my visits to the hospice would one day land on my own doorstep. Well it did, and when it happened it hit me hard.

Rachel discovered a lump on her breast and went to the doctor's to have it checked out. She was sent away not once, but three times, having been told there was nothing to worry about. We didn't agree and persisted, finally persuading a reluctant doctor to make an appointment for Rachel at Clatterbridge Hospital on the Wirral. It was as a non-urgent case and could have been at any time within the upcoming eight weeks!

Fortunately, Rachel got a cancellation inside a fortnight and we arrived promptly for the appointment. I must give special mention to all the nurses and doctors at Clatterbridge Hospital. They were really supportive to us in our hour of need. They had all the time in the world for us, and let us ask as many questions as we wanted. Rachel went down the corridor for a scan, leaving me to wait in reception. She had only been away for a few minutes when she came back towards me, followed by a nurse, who told us that the doctor wanted a chat. We were told that the lump may be benign, but that it could also be cancerous. Cancer – the very word fills you with dread. The doctor added that he wanted to do a biopsy to remove some cells for further examination, and then send them off for analysis to see how far, if at all, the cancer had spread through Rachel's body. The results would be back in a fortnight.

Well, you can make up your own mind as to how long that fortnight lasted. Two weeks seemed like two years. We asked ourselves hundreds of questions. We had sleepless nights when neither of us dared to mention the possibility that the disease could be rife through Rachel's body. We decided to close ranks and confide in each other. The kids did not need to know anything at this stage. The wonderful Rachel never once complained about what was going on. She just continued with everyday life for the sake of the children, who needed her. Her attitude was that crying wouldn't help. This matter-of-fact approach is the way that Rachel deals with most things in life, and that is why I am full of admiration and love for her.

The test results eventually returned and we were told that the cancer was at grade one, which meant that it had not spread far, thank God. Rachel went back into hospital to have the tumour removed and to start a five-week course of radiotherapy. She went to Clatterbridge every day for those five weeks, and has also had to take tablets for the last five years. She goes back for regular scans and will have to have annual mammogram checks for the next five years or so but, touch wood, everything seems to be fine. Although we'd had concerns about the way in which Rachel was treated when we first flagged it up, we decided not to take things further and moved on. Since then, we have been delighted to do some work for the Lily Centre, a self-financing breast cancer support group in Liverpool.

Rachel understands me. She is a mother, a wife and a friend. I'll grow old and grey with her. We have had to support each other through difficult, life-threatening times, and it has brought us closer together. I have had a few bob in my time, and lost a few, but Rachel has not had the chance to benefit. That is one of the main reasons why I am trying to make something of all my experience and qualifications. I want Rachel to benefit from what I achieve in the future.

If you stopped a hundred people on the Wirral and mentioned Eric Nixon to them, I wonder how many would think immediately of Elvis? As a born entertainer I have enjoyed putting a smile on people's faces with my act and I've been doing it for some years now, raising a lot of cash for charity in the process. The 'King' is my hero and I can confidently say that I'm the only Elvis Presley impersonator with a Class 'A' coaching badge! Many have commented that I'm a better goalkeeper than an Elvis, but my act goes down well and the family like to come and watch – and I love doing it. I've got the white suit, the high collar and the flared trousers and do lots of charity gigs, as well as weddings. I get out there, sing the songs and make the stage my own. I have my own PA system and backing tracks and I aim to be professional because people pay to watch. I've even performed on the pitch at Prenton Park! Sometimes I branch out and do some of the New Romantic stuff such as Spandau Ballet. I'm also extending the Elvis act to freshen it up by doing a separate set from the 'GI Blues' period! I call the show 'Viva Las Nico'! There are two 40-minute slots, one with my original stuff and the other the army image.

It started in Magaluf, then Eddie Bishop and I went head-to-head not too long ago at a former players function, just as we had all those years ago in Majorca! Stevie Mungall had a testimonial do at the Primrose in Bebington. We all decided what we were going to do, and I went for a medallion man look in an Elvis costume. Soon after I started as a patron at Clare House and did the charity stuff. People are always asking me if I get nervous up on stage but I tell them that I've been making an idiot of myself in front of much bigger crowds for more years than I care to remember, so let's go for it!

I've always fancied myself as a singer and enjoyed a few sing-songs at the club, led by George Wilson. George had come to Tranmere as the fitness coach in 2000. I got on well with him. On away trips to London or East Anglia, George would bring his guitar and we would sing along after a few beers. I remember one occasion when we were due to play at Norwich the next day. George went and brought his guitar down. Dave Watson and Les Parry joined us and we had a fantastic time bashing out the hits. Dave enjoyed it so much that he still mentions it every time our paths cross.

Chapter Twenty Four

THE ART OF KEEPING

'I am not a natural but made myself into a goalkeeper at the top level through hard work'

I study the art of goalkeeping as closely now as I did when I was busting a gut to get into the Manchester City team. There's nothing more pleasurable than seeing a young, fresh-faced keeper learning from my experience and making progress.

It does not replace playing, but coaching goalkeepers is the next best thing. Young players today have something that we never had, and I know I've banged on about this in the book. Goalkeeping coaches are now part and parcel of the game, but it has taken some time since the likes of big Joe Corrigan preached about the need to have specialists to support this most individual and unique of positions. Every young apprentice, whatever his trade, needs a mentor and it's good to see how many of the players I once faced are now passing on their experience at clubs across the land. Mike Stowell is with

Leicester City, Martyn Margetson, my understudy at Manchester City, is at West Ham United whilst Kevin Pressman, whose injury gave me that final bit of action at Hillsborough, is at Bradford City.

To the outsider, goalkeeping is no doubt a straightforward and simple business that hasn't changed since Adam was a lad kicking a ball round the Garden of Eden. You have to stand between some sticks and stop a ball from going across a line. Well, that couldn't be further from the truth because goalkeepers in the modern era need to dictate the way a game is played far more than ever before and to do so requires awareness, skill and understanding. Many used to say that you had to be daft to be a goalkeeper. Not anymore!

The advent of the back-pass rule has undoubtedly widened the scope of the keeper's duties. This change in the laws took place in the early 1990s. As much as anything it was to discourage time-wasting and defensive play and the new rule stated that if a ball was intentionally passed back to the goalkeeper he was not allowed to pick it up with his hands.

The keeper's role changed overnight. Suddenly there was a need to be able to kick or pass a moving ball upfield off either foot which, in turn, put greater emphasis on trusting the quality of the playing surface. What often happens is that the ball gets passed back when a full-back or the centre-half is being chased down and has run out of other options. How many times does the poor old keeper get it nice and early and with plenty of time to make the best use of it?!

Developments have made it increasingly necessary for a goalkeeper to be able to read the game and communicate with his back-line when calling for the back-pass. The goalkeeper now has more chances to start a new period of play, get his defence moving around him and be seen as a sweeper – playing the ball along the carpet, starting moves from the back and understanding team-mates' strengths and weaknesses.

What I keep telling my young keepers is that they must not let the game pass them by, and that they should use every situation to their advantage. I deliver the messages with a lot of the banter which has been part of my make-up through my life on and off the pitch. I always have a laugh and a joke with the young ones about what I have achieved and they pull my leg, but at the same time they show respect because they know where I have been and what I have done. Equally, I have respect for the young professionals plying their trade.

When the likes of Andy Dibble and Perry Suckling come along you could easily be dead and buried, unless you do something for yourself and fight tooth and nail to build a career. I know from bitter experience how difficult it can be and really feel for the new breed facing the same obstacles. I have every admiration for the young goalkeepers who are prepared to graft and, having experienced situations like that, I am well-placed to advise. The more you play this game of football, the more you realise that you have to stand up for yourself or otherwise others will just kick you to the kerb.

They know that I am not talking rubbish because of where I have played and for how long. I can use my experience of the highs and lows without giving them the feeling that I am a show-off. Having gone through the pain of being dropped or hearing fans shouting for your blood can only help you with young keepers as they come to terms with similar situations in their own careers. When something goes wrong, they usually have a tendency to want to run round the block 15 times and up the ante. That's their way of reacting and, to be honest, I have done that myself – no one told me how to react to adversity. I can now categorically state that pumping more iron is not the answer. It is time to relax, take stock of the situation and start to force your way back in.

Taking training sessions always requires careful thought and planning. It's not just about kicking ball after ball at the keeper. When I was at Fleetwood Town I would visualise the session in my mind as I drove up the motorway from the Wirral. Practicing kicking technique can be a particular problem because of limited space. I have to think about what we have got available and how to combat it. Some days we would be at Fylde Rugby Club in Lytham St Annes and on others we'd be at the main ground in Fleetwood, where the layout and space available would be different. I had to adapt my methods to suit but I always made sure to hit the ground running, getting sessions going nice and early. We would be all muddied up before the prima-donnas had even left the warmth of the changing rooms! I started training early when I first went to Manchester City and it is a habit that I have happily stuck to.

There's another crucial lesson that I pass on. If you don't look after yourself as a keeper, you're gone. I never took a day off work and avoided the distractions presented to me in my early days learning the game. I was driven on by the fact that I was not a natural goalkeeper, but manufactured after that all-important change of position at school from being a centre-forward who liked to bang the goals in. Inspired by Joe Corrigan, who was the same height and the same build, I made myself into a goalkeeper at the top level through sheer hard work and dedication. When we arrived at a base before the games, Tranmere trainer Kenny Jones and I would immediately look for a patch of grass behind the hotel where we would work on a series of exercises designed to get my body tuned up and in shape.

I've had plenty of time to assess what makes a good keeper. The need to be brave is right up there, along with having agility and reflexes. The best keepers also have a clear understanding of the game and how diverse it can be.

There are goalkeepers and shot-stoppers. My old mate, Neville Southall, is the best type of shot-stopper I've seen. You would never see him coming for crosses or anticipating things before they happen. Nev would rely on pure reflex action to make saves, the type of saves that, on many occasions, would make the difference between winning and losing. He was a popular figure across the Mersey at Goodison Park and I remember a poll that was done a few years back by 'Football Focus' on the BBC. Nev was voted the all-time cult hero at Everton with 74% of the votes, with Alan Ball way back in second place with 14%! It's always great to see a goalie getting recognition, even though one fan wrote 'his exceptional ability between the sticks was only surpassed by his exceptional inability to smile!'

The opposite type of keeper would be Bruce Grobbelaar at Liverpool. Bruce would come for balls that he had no right to get. It was an approach that brought much success, but it was also risky and he would make mistakes. Fortunately for him, he had a fantastic team around him and the likes of Alan Hansen and Phil Neil would usually mop up.

It is for others to judge but, in my opinion, I was both a shot-stopper and a goalkeeper. My game was based on communicating messages simply and clearly. My approach was short, sharp, bright and, to quote Tony Book, 'bushy-tailed'! If I was standing next to you and dropped a ball, I would want you to be on to it straight away. There's no time to think, just react to it immediately.

I admired many of the keepers who I played opposite, and feel privileged to count a lot of them as my friends to this day. Tony Coton, who's now coaching in Dubai, was brilliant. I played against him at Watford and when he came to City. I always compared myself to guys like Tony because I spent years playing at the same level. To be honest, there was never a time when I felt second-rate by comparison. I worked hard to make sure that never happened.

In the modern game there's none better than Joe Hart and I'm delighted that my old club, Manchester City, have one of the finest home-grown talents. Ben Foster at West Brom is another good young professional. These days I don't think English keepers get a fair crack of the whip. There are foreign players in the game who get chance after chance, and if our keepers had made the same number of mistakes their feet wouldn't touch the ground. Ben Amos, at Manchester United, is a typical example of someone who's having to be patient. There's a feeling that you always have to bring goalkeepers, and coaches, in from abroad. Foreign managers bring their own coaches in with them. Why isn't there more faith in our own talents? Amos is an outstanding prospect from Macclesfield whose route is blocked at Old Trafford by not one, but two, foreign goalkeepers in David de Gea and Anders Lindegaard. Flying the flag for our own talent is a subject that I care passionately about. Now it's time to put the soap box away!

Chapter Twenty Five

THIS IS IT

'I am always being told that you get out of the game what you put in. I don't agree'

Hillsborough welcomed me with rapturous applause as I left the bench and crossed the white line on to the turf of one of the most famous grounds in the football world. One week short of my 41st birthday, I was back on a football pitch. Body ravaged by a football lifetime of hard training, I must have been the first player in the history of football to limp on to the pitch.

I really should not have been there in the first place. I had joined the club to help coach their goalkeepers, but ended up on the bench for the home game against Grimsby Town. The youngsters had all been sidelined for one reason or another and only regular keeper Kevin Pressman stood between me and a dramatic return.

To be honest, I did not expect to get any action as it does not usually happen that way for keepers warming the bench. But would you believe it – 25 minutes or so in, and Kevin suffered a hand injury which meant that he had to come off. All sorts of thoughts ran through my mind as I replaced him, but one kept coming back: 'What the hell am I doing here?'

Minutes later the ball was played in and picked up by a Grimsby player, who had been causing us problems all afternoon. My situation was not helped by the centre-halves going missing. He was bearing down into the area one-on-one, no doubt fancying his chances against the old guy. The situation was 60-40 in his favour, and I had a big decision to make...

I was 40 years old with a career behind me against a talented kid. How do I play it? Within a few seconds, a lifetime of experience came to the surface and the real Eric Nixon came out. Like so often in my career, I went for it and attacked the moment. He got stretchered off the pitch while I stayed on, and kept a clean sheet!

It was ironic that my last ever game involved someone leaving the field injured by me because 18 years ago, almost to the day, I had clobbered a defender in my first game. I was fulfilling the dream of playing for Manchester City, my home-town club, and Kenny Clements copped for it.

In between, I played over 650 times for 14 clubs. There were massive highs, such as 30,000 City fans chanting my name at Wembley and unbearable lows, when abuse from the fans made me doubt whether I wanted to continue playing at all.

And now, with my career over, I am facing perhaps my greatest challenge – forging a life beyond football. I am approaching 50 and facing up to 40 years in 'retirement'. It is a long time to last without the banter and the adrenalin rushes that made me feel so privileged to have played the game I love.

I am always being told that you only get out of the game what you put into it. I don't agree. I definitely put in more than I got out. Had I been playing today it would have been totally different. There are players now who are prepared to sit on the bench and collect millions for doing nothing. I dedicated a lot of hard work and hours to being a professional footballer. If I had played just one game I would have felt fortunate so you can imagine how much I appreciate having had the chance to play over 600 matches at all levels.

However, the type of person I was during my career is definitely holding me back now. It's stopped me from moving forward. The fights in the tunnel, telling people the way it is... because I'm larger than life, I've never normally got second best. But it's all worked against me since I retired from playing.

Through all the ups and downs, I constantly think of the part that my dad would have played had he survived longer than the all-too-early age of 38. I have missed him so much and I know that he would have been so proud of my achievements. Family values that he and mum created live on, though, and are as important today as they were when I was a kid growing up on the streets of Manchester.

I constantly look back through my life and feel blessed to have had a mum and dad who gave me a secure upbringing. From childhood through to the present day, my family life has been so precious to me. The values and lessons learned back in Harpurhey and Withington from loving parents have stood me in good stead ever since, and I never miss out on the chance to return to my past and recall its many happy moments, as well as learn from its more bitter experiences. I feel fortunate to have shared so many happy times with my four brothers, and we still live close and keep in touch.

There is no doubt that the support of my family has allowed

me to make my mark on a game that I have loved playing from when I was a kid, and I am proud of what I have achieved. Not many can say that they have had the chance to pull on the shirt for their local team at the highest level, and to captain another team at Wembley. I can honestly say that there is nothing that I would change. I've had to cope with lows when my form has dipped and the fans have got on to me, but there have been many more highs.

I am respected by the majority in football as a fine keeper and a leader of men, but there are others who see me as a 6ft 4ins man-mountain who would threaten to pull your throat out given half a chance. There is no doubt that I had my moments and did things that I would later regret. I came through a tough upbringing in the local Manchester leagues, and always wore my heart on my sleeve. I was a winner through and through, but this mentality never stopped me shaking an opponent's hand or buying him a pint after the game. I gave my all in training and matches to convert myself from a budding centre-forward to a high-class goalkeeper.

As a person, I think that I have grown up a lot. Many lessons have been learned. The abrasive young pro who took a situation by the scruff of the neck is very much a person of the past. I can now sit back and reflect. Like a good wine, I've matured with age and am trying hard to carve a serious and meaningful future for myself. I've gone out and worked my butt off to give myself the best chance possible to make my mark after football in the way I did when I played. It'll happen eventually because I'm not a quitter!

Mention Eric Nixon to people and many will still see me as the joker in the pack who is never happy unless he is at the centre of things with a drink in his hand. This has definitely been the case over many years, but those close to me will tell you that there is definitely another side to Nico! If I walk into a crowded room today, I'm quite happy to sit and mind my own business whereas before I would have wanted to make an impact straight away. People will look my way because of my height and size but if they don't know me or need me then that's fine. If they recognise me, however, and if someone wants to engage me in conversation or a bit of banter then 'bang', I am happy to be what people want me to be.

I never get far these days, particularly on the Wirral, without someone making contact, usually a greeting of some sort. I once met a set of supporters on a station platform. They were dressed as superheroes and did a double-take as I walked past before launching into a chorus of ,'There's only one Eric Nixon!' That kind of reaction always brings a smile to my face, and I'd give some back. Then there's the kind of adulation that, quite frankly, is a bit embarrassing. I was in a chippy one night, on my way home at the end of a long day, when some guy recognised me and wouldn't let it drop. He grabbed my arm and stopped me moving on whilst he went on about how good I was. In his eyes I was apparently better than Southall and Schmeichal put together! He was right of course, but I just wanted a pie and the chance to eat it at home!

Most people I meet are great and I appreciate it, but there are occasionally others who are more uncomplimentary and I have to accept at those moments that I was the larger-than-life cocky character who rubbed some people up the wrong way. Football fans can have long memories.

My family and I are very happy on the Wirral and Rachel and I have made some very special friends during our time here. I have survived two major health scares and nursed my lovely wife through her own trauma. These experiences have made me determined to appreciate even more what I have got, and explains why I give so much time to charity work.

As I drove back home on that Friday afternoon after cleaning Gary Bailey's car, I saw an opportunity and went for it. The rest, as they say, is history. Since then, I've seen the world and played at great stadiums such as Old Trafford, Anfield, Wembley and, of course, Maine Road against many of the game's best such as Dalglish and Keegan. Two titanium knees are a price worth paying for following the game that I have loved since kicking a ball along the narrow streets of Manchester.

I've enjoyed every step of the way, particularly the chance to entertain the fans who give us a living. I've worked as long as I can, as hard as I can and as fast as I can to be the strongest, the most efficient, the fastest, the most agile. As a manufactured goalkeeper, there was no other way to go about it in order to catch up and stay at my peak. That's how I wanted it to be, and others will decide how far I got to achieving all that.

Fate certainly leant a hand when my old primary school teacher, Mr O'Hara, converted me from centre-forward to goalkeeper but, in truth, there was no better position for me – goalkeepers are unique!

You also have to have a streak of madness running through you. It is a position that has enabled me to show-off, draw attention to myself and wear the 'Number 1' shirt.

Big Eric couldn't have played anywhere else, could he?

How others see 'Nico'

WHAT THEY SAY

'If ever you want an opinion, he will give you his – and yours as well!'

Les Parry

Tranmere Rovers manager (2009-)

Eric and I came to Tranmere at about the same time. He was already on the scene when I took the position as part-time physio in July 1991, and he had just led the team to glory in the Division Three play-off final against Bolton Wanderers.

Signing Eric had been a big gamble for Rovers manager, Johnny King, because he had a reputation for fighting in his time at Manchester City, and it was also a big financial gamble for a club like Tranmere to make. The captain's role was always going to happen because Kingy liked that type who led from the front. Nico was an exceptional shot-stopper and had all the other attributes you need as a goalkeeper, but it was what he brought to the game that stood him out.

He marshalled the back four and the team in a way that the club had not seen before. He could be at the players all the time, even in training. You quickly learned not to take the mick out of him on the training ground because he would be after you! If he'd been a quiet and retiring guy he would still have been a good keeper, but not nearly as effective. To have someone like him around the dressing room was brilliant. If there was trouble on or off the pitch Eric would always be the first to get involved and back up the lads. I think that his style made him enemies before he came to Tranmere, but I honestly cannot remember anything like that at Prenton Park.

Eric had a big character to go with his big physique. When he went in to talk to Johnny King about his second contract he came out bragging about how he'd been offered wheelbarrow loads of cash to stay! The other lads were joking with him, hoping there was enough left in the pot for them!

There's no doubt that he played a massive part in the Tranmere Rovers success story. He'll tell you that he was the main man and that they built a statue of him at Cammell Laird! If I had a tenner for every time I've heard that!

I've known Eric for 20 years and spent a massive amount of time with him. I can honestly say that I know him better than most, having had the chance to accompany him to theatre with my camera as he underwent knee surgery! I have been close by as he's cheated death on two occasions, and been delighted to see him bounce back.

Nico has been a huge part of the Merseyside football scene for many a year, which isn't a bad achievement for someone from Manchester! I was chuffed to bits for him when he was awarded the Liverpool Echo's Dixie Dean award for services to football on Merseyside because he did so much to put Tranmere on the football map and show that Merseyside had three clubs, not two.

He's one of the best mates a guy could have. He would do anything for you and you can always guarantee that he will bring a smile to your face.

Steve Mungall
Tranmere Rovers defender (1979-1996)

I remember a game at West Ham. It was getting towards the end and we were 1-0 down. I passed back to Nico, albeit on his left foot. As the ball came to him, Tony Cottee was closing him down. Instead of hoofing it clear with his left foot he thought he'd be like Maradona and take it round Cottee. Cottee took the ball off him and Nico had to bring him down to stop him scoring. Julian Dicks duly slotted the ball home from the penalty spot.

None of it was Nico's fault, of course. He blamed me for the back-pass! I said: "All you needed to do was welly it instead of being a smart-ass and take it past him." Well, it got heated in the dressing room and the boys eventually had to separate us. I took my life in my hands that day because there was only going to be one winner! We were so committed to winning games, though. Nico was still the first to buy me a drink when we went up to the bar afterwards. This typified the great team spirit. Differences were soon forgotten and there were no grudges or cliques. We were more a family than a football team.

Nico always had a great sense of humour. He reckoned he could have played longer but it was a bad back that put him out from all the years that he carried us!

He often came across as the big 'I am' with lots of bravado, but behind that was a very caring person.

He looked after everybody. If any of the boys were in trouble Nico would be the first to jump in and help them. Anyone who thought he was just big-headed and loud didn't know him.

Shaun Garnett
Tranmere Rovers defender (1987-1996)

I first met Eric in 1987 when he came on loan and I was an apprentice. I'd never seen a goalkeeper that big – he was built like a brick shit-house! When you saw him in training you knew that he was better than anything we'd had previously. We were all aware that he had come from a big club.

He was perhaps the first big name that we had attracted to Tranmere and he was, of course, followed by others as the team became more successful. Normally, the likes of Liverpool and Everton would have signed that sort of player but, because of the financial backing from Mr Johnson, networking and recruitment at the club got bigger.

It was an instant fix for us as keepers had come and gone and we needed stability at the back. Nico arrived and there was your answer.

It doesn't matter what position you play. As long as you're a communicator you can skipper from anywhere, and Nico was just that. He barked out instructions and his big personality forced itself on the game to such an extent that he often turned lost causes into victories. He could not impose his captaincy in terms of tackles around the pitch or shots on goal, but his sheer presence counted just as much.

You have to be careful what you say about him, because he gets big-headed, but he was a very important part of the Tranmere success story. A Manchester lad coming to Merseyside was not normal, but Nico's manner and humour made him like one of us. He settled and blended and made many friends.

I was originally his boot boy so I have always had a special connection with the big man. He has always been a massive help to me, and I've learnt my trade through him. He still gives me advice now that I'm in coaching and I appreciate it.

We've enjoyed some brilliant times. He's great company and not shy when he gets on the mike! I've been to some of his gigs and he's good. He's got the costumes and the audience join in. Eric's a very loyal friend. If he likes you you've got a great mate, but there are no grey areas with him. He's tried a few things since he packed in and probably gets bored easily needing a new challenge.

Eddie Bishop
Tranmere Rovers midfielder (1987-1990)

Eric hasn't changed as long as I've known him. He was a fantastic keeper, great to have in the dressing room and a bundle of fun. When he came on loan he was a big name for a club who were just on the up in the old Fourth Division. There was a piece missing and Eric filled that gap. He was a big presence and everyone warmed to him. He was a great shot-stopper and for a big guy he was very agile. He helped to give the team a strong spine along with the likes of Mark Hughes, Steve Vickers and Shaun Garnett.

Dave Challinor
Tranmere Rovers defender (1996-2001)

Nico was in goal when I made my first-team debut. He was a massive help to a young kid coming through. In fact, all the senior players went out of their way to help, which was one reason why the club was such a good one to play for. There was bundles of spirit and there still is today when we meet up. He plays his part in getting the former players together. Much of it has been down to his initiative.

Ged Brannan
Tranmere Rovers defender/midfielder (1990-1997)
Eric is one of the best goalkeepers that I've ever played with. His handling and shot-stopping made him a top, top keeper, as well as a showman! I came to Tranmere as a YTS player and he took me under his wing. He made everyone feel welcome and broke the ice many a time. He is in many ways Mr Tranmere, and he's done a massive amount for my career.

Kenny Irons
Tranmere Rovers midfielder (1989-1999)
Eric was a top goalkeeper, big and strong with a shot-stopping ability up with the best. I was an apprentice at the time he came from City. Eric will tell you that he was a snip at 60 grand, but I thought he was overpriced! Seriously, Nico did not disappoint, although you could never go near him because he was always angry! We've shared some tremendous times, on and off the field.

John McGreal
Tranmere Rovers defender (1991-1999)
Nico always had something to say to the youngsters like me. His banter got you involved straight away and he showed you a lot of respect. I remember when the new back-pass rule came into play. Johnny Morrissey would shout 'Shields' – a signal that the spectators had better watch out as Big Eric tried to hoof a moving ball downfield!

Micky Mellon
Tranmere Rovers midfielder (1997-2004),
Fleetwood Town manager (2008-)

Eric had a massive presence. You always knew that he was around. He was a terrific keeper and when he came to Blackpool on loan, make no mistake, he was still one of the best around and knew play-off situations well.

He was one of a number of people who put Tranmere where they are today. There had an unbelievable team spirit and belief – and Eric was at the heart of that. There was also a brilliant youth policy, which paid dividends.

Eric has a massive heart and has always been as honest as the day is long. People knew where they stood with him. He would stick up for one of his own if he felt that there was a wrong to put right, and if backed into a corner he would defend himself.

He is a thinker who wants to get something going for himself either inside or outside the game which is commendable. He's not had the best of luck so far but if there were medals given for trying he would be up there on the podium.

He's always an entertainer, and I worry sometimes that he thinks he's Elvis! He's a great mate, though.

Paul Linwood
Tranmere Rovers defender (2003-2006)

Eric was still a player when I was a YTS, and a coach when I turned professional. I was a Tranmere supporter before I joined the club and Eric was a bit of a superstar to me and my mates. He was a real character and the fans flocked to see him.

I remember a pre-season friendly when one of their guys went down. Nico was straight out, counting him out like a boxing referee! We used to love the tricks before the game, spinning a ball on his hand and his neck were two of them. All for show!

Eric was a brilliant keeper and many have wondered why he didn't play international football.

When John Aldridge became manager he needed people he could trust around him and went for Nico as goalkeeping coach. He played for the reserves a few times when he was coach, and I played in front of him as I started my own career. My first game was at Prenton Park against Birmingham City and he never shut up for the whole match!

You wouldn't want to make a mistake because he'd let you know and even with dodgy knees he could run fast to catch you for a word or two!

When he was out on the beer, Eric could make pints look like shots but he was good value, one of the most confident men that I've ever met. He would do rubbish tricks involving coins and cups over and over again!

A lot of people think he loves himself but it is an act. He will go out of his way to help people. That's something a lot of people don't see and realise. People say that you need diplomas and degrees to be successful these days, and Eric has gone out and got his fair share of qualifications. But there's no better degree than having the experience of playing over 600 league games. That sort of experience is priceless.

Nico would have got a degree for winding people up! Every day he would be on at Jason McAteer, the former Liverpool player, who was at the club as a player between 2004 and 2007 and later as assistant to John Barnes in 2009. Eric would have a go at him about never winning a trophy when he had won loads! He'd go on about the Wembley trips. Jason's reply was to mention playing in the Premier League, but Eric would just laugh back, happy that he had got Jason going!

Steve Macauley
Manchester City defender (1985-1989),
Fleetwood Town coach (2008-)

A lot of people got Nico wrong. For a person who many saw as a bully, he had a soft interior and was a well-grounded person who would give you the shirt off his back. If there is what you might call a 'bullying side', it is his way of getting the best out of people. He was also never far from the scene when there was a scrape!

As a keeper, he was a shot-stopper and as fit as a flea. He was perhaps not at his best on the deck, but good in every other respect. Nico was a winner. He would never accept second-best. That was innate within him and not something you can instill.

As a football coach, he is top drawer. The experience that he can pass on is huge. You can't buy it. That was shown at Fleetwood when we had the two best keepers in the league. Eric was very protective of them, calling them 'my keepers'. He is a deep thinker and a scholar of the game.

It was great to work alongside him again after all these years and, believe me, we heard all the stories from his Tranmere days countless times! He has sung Elvis over and over and done his coin trick on me about 3,000 times – I still haven't spotted how he did it!

He's a great mate and I'll never forget one of his catch phrases: 'Never knock off!'

Scott Davies
Fleetwood Town goalkeeper (2010-)

Nico was already at Fleetwood Town when I came down from Morecambe. I had heard a lot about him before we met. When we did he was straight into the Wembley banter, but I've been there as well, in a play-off for Morecambe, so I could throw that back at him! He always wanted the last word though and, straight away, he would add that he'd been there eight times!

When he first coached me he told me I was working too hard, which I took on board. He has always been a fit character and got where he did through hard work, but I know he feels he pushed it too hard and is paying the price now with his knees.

When you've reached 24 it's not about technique because you've got where you've got because it is sound. With Nico, he tweaked my game and made me a more mature player. On match days he was brilliant, making sure he focused on positives at half-time because I still had another 45 minutes to go.

He would deal with the areas for improvement on the training ground cleverly, always knowing just how much to say and keeping things going with none-stop chat and banter! I always took his advice seriously because he had been there.

He was brilliant when I was dropped. Although he needed to look after Danny Hurst, the number one, he made sure that he also looked after the number two keeper. Again, he has experienced that himself.

If I can achieve half of what he has in his career in the number of games and seasons that he has stayed at the top I will be well pleased.

Danny Hurst
Fleetwood Town goalkeeper (2008-2011),
Barrow goalkeeper (2011-)

I remember my first meeting with Nico. He had come to watch a game at Fleetwood prior to starting as coach. He strode into the dressing room and introduced himself to me: "Hi, I'm Eric Nixon and I'm starting the game tonight!" I began to laugh.

He asked what was so funny, then just walked off! I wondered what the heck all this was about but soon realised that this was the nature of the man.

I must have heard about virtually every game he's played. We'd be on the coach and a match would come on the television. He'd ask me if I'd played at that ground. I'd reply: "You know I haven't, Nico." He would be straight back: "I've only played there about 10 times!"

He would work you hard in training and we'd always be out well before the rest of the lads. He would have us caked in mud and sweat before they'd even started! We would work hard and laugh our heads off all the time. Nico, Scott and me would always finish with a penalty shoot-out, which I always won!

You would come off the pitch at half time or after a game and reckon you'd done well, but he would always pick up on a couple of things. Over the years those little things have helped my game and taken me up a couple of levels to where I wanted to be. Nico was always on the phone when I was recovering from injury and I guarantee that I would always put it down feeling more positive and with a grin on my face. That was the effect that he had.

Andy Quayle
Tranmere Rovers groundsman (1985-)

Even though City was the love of his life, there's no doubt that Eric was a massive part of Tranmere Rovers. Attendances rocketed with the promotions and Wembley trips, and he was one of half-a-dozen key signings. I remember him living in a flat up by the Bowler Hat in Oxton and marrying a local girl.

With all the Friday night games and the goals being shown on 'Saint and Greavsie' I think that Rovers became a lot of fans' second favourite team.

Eric was definitely larger than life, always wanting to be the centre of attention. It was great to have someone like him leading the club on and off the pitch and he was definitely a fans' favourite. He could be a big-headed bugger, though! I took a lot of stick from him over the years – he'd slaughter the pitch and slaughter me – but it was always good natured banter!

Andy Doyle, former ticket office manager, chairman of the Tranmere Rovers Supporters' Association, founder member of the Tranmere and Wirral Supporters' Trust, current Rovers reporter for BBC Radio Merseyside

I've followed Rovers since I was four-years-old, and Eric has been one of the largest characters in the club's history. He's a comedian with a smile never far from his face and there's always a word for everyone. He's always held true to Rovers and I remember that it was a huge deal when he first arrived. I was shopping in Birkenhead Market at the time. My mum and I were at a stall which sold foreign produce. There was a radio on and I suddenly picked up some breaking news that there was an announcement imminent from Tranmere.

My attention was suddenly captured. Anything to do with Rovers I wanted to know about. I asked the stall holder to turn the radio up and heard that the club had signed Eric Nixon. Mum always maintains that she got no sense out of me after that! I dragged her back to the car with only half the shopping done so that I could get up to the ground. There were hundreds of people milling around the car park. Eric had made history by playing in all four divisions in one season, and suddenly we had a household name at Prenton Park!

For the three years covering the Wembley trips my job as ticket office manager entitled me to a seat on the team coach alongside the great Johnny King. I witnessed Eric's fondness for a practical joke on many an occasion, including the time he moved Albert's bus while he was at the loo!

Eric was also famous for his Elvis bits and pieces and I know he enjoys doing the shows and often raising money for charity. I remember him appearing on a stage somewhere in full garb soon after arriving at the club, thinking that this guy isn't from the normal mould! Go to any pub on the Wirral now and mention Eric Nixon and they'll say, 'Don't you mean Elvis?'

He was an entertainer, and I think it was all part of wanting to be liked. As a player, Eric was a man-mountain who controlled his area. Johnny King had clearly decided that he needed to avoid his side leaking goals and as soon as he got his keeper and back line sorted the team moved forward. When Eric comes charging out you close your eyes and expect a crash! There is a long list of strikers, and Tranmere defenders, who can testify to that. He will shout "Keeper!" and that fist will shoot out like Superman's. On more than one occasion he has found a chin rather than the ball!

Eric's passion for the club was sensed by the fans and was well-illustrated in the play-off semi-final, second leg against Leicester City in 1994. There was a mass brawl in Tranmere's half of the pitch. Out of the corner of your eye you're suddenly aware of this purple-shirted figure moving out of his area and heading downfield. You just knew that someone was heading for an unhappy evening!

On his arrival, the players in the group seemed to part like the Red Sea and he got the wrong man, pushing Simon Grayson over! He was looking for David Speedie. The ref showed red and Eric walked without argument, stopping only to have a brief eyeball 'chat' with a Leicester player on the way!

Despite the controversy, Rovers always tried to do things the right way. We regularly came across teams who cried, harassed and cheated. Others felt the need to use the wrong tactics.

Eric had seen the big lights in his career and went down the leagues to become a better player. It shows what the lower levels can offer. He was certainly a main factor in turning Rovers' fortunes round. It was not just about what he could bring to the table, but signing players of that calibre made it easier to sign others. Eric started the big wheel turning and that is something that he can be proud of. Other big names followed like Pat Nevin, Shaun Teale and, of course, John Aldridge. I seem to remember reading in a book, perhaps Howard Kendall's, that his biggest regret was not signing Aldridge when he came back from Spain. Tranmere got him and what a deal that was!

Eric will always call a spade a spade. If you ever want an opinion, he will give you his – and yours as well! That's what is so lovable about him. There are no 'ifs, buts and maybes' with him. He lives the life in front of him. He will tell you if you are wrong, whether you wanted to hear or not. Put 'Yes men' in front of him and the shutters come down. He will not want to know.

He was and is a winner. That's what he has tried through his life and I am not sure it has always come off. When you get to know and understand the guy you learn not to take it to heart. That is his style.

If you had not seen him for 10 years and then bumped into him, the reaction would be the same as if he had seen you yesterday. Out would come the big hand and there would be a cheery greeting.

Keith Nethercott
Best Man

I watched my fiancee's son, Matt, play football every Sunday. At 16 he was floating balls in off either foot. Knowing they had a growing youth academy, I asked Eric what chance there would be of getting him to Fleetwood Town. He took me to a game and chatted with the coach, who said: "Bring him down Monday." He went for a trial – and he's not been back since! The move has changed the kid's life. He absolutely loves it and it was all down to Eric. He didn't ask for anything, he just got on with it and did the business. That's Eric all over.

Dave Faulkner
Sponsor and friend

Eric always impressed me with his will to win. He didn't take any prisoners during the game, and was known to race the length of the Tranmere pitch to sort a situation out. But he also took time out for handicapped supporters, always making a special fuss of them before and after a game. That had an effect on me and is what prompted me to sponsor him because I thought that it was good that he had time for other people.

Eric has a big pair of hands and a very big heart. He would always help others. When I had bowel cancer a couple of years ago, he was very attentive. Nothing was too much trouble. He came and spoke to us in Rotary and his Elvis went down a storm on a number of occasions at Bromborough Golf Club.

Steve Roper
Chairman of Former Players' Foundation

I was working in Liverpool and coming back up Singleton Avenue on the bus on a Friday night. I noticed a gang of people at Prenton Park. I told my mum that I didn't want any tea and went straight down to see what was happening. I was about 16 and I've been following Rovers ever since.

Eric was the keeper who filled the goal. I remember that he was very vocal. He spread himself out to his full extent, and was not frightened to come out and get hurt. I can only think of Peter Schmeichel as a comparison in size and the way he played the game. The banter was always there with the fans. With him being keeper, there was that opportunity for a closer relationship with the supporters behind the goal.

Andy Donnelly and Margaret O'Hare
Tranmere Rovers supporters

Eric was definitely one of the most popular players. I remember five or six years ago we spotted him in Gran Canaria airport. Andy said: "There's Eric Nixon by the carousel!" I replied: "It can't be! He wouldn't be on the same plane as us!" He was very approachable and we had a chat.

He's tried all sorts since he left football. There was the 'Blue Monkey' car wash and the Elvis shows. Peter Johnson and Johnny King had a big influence on the success of the team, and Ian Muir's goals got them rewards. But Eric was right there – a strong character – and we needed one to guide us.

Alan Nixon, brother

I always took the father-figure role seriously after dad died. I was a bit distanced from the rest, like the boss. I remember dad taking us for some shoes across Platt Lane. We went over the bridge and I was walking 100 yards ahead of the rest. As the oldest, I got the new clothes and my own bedroom so there were perks!

I was a massive Man City supporter and would go to the matches as a kid with friends such as Terry Lynch, Dave Trimble and Manny, whose son Jason Manford has gone on to make a good living out of Mancunian humour! After dad died I went over to United!

I would go to support Eric home and away when he played for Old Moat and Manchester Boys. Mum was a very proud lady. She never asked for anything off anyone. Times have not always been rosy for her, but she has always been there for us. It was a happy upbringing. No complaints.

We were all pretty grounded regarding Eric's fame. I remember shouting like mad on his first-team debut, but he did not hear me. Mum went to that match, even though she was blind as a bat.

A lot of my mates went from Manchester to watch the Tranmere Rovers matches when they played at Wembley. They were big days out for all of us. The Full Members Cup final for Manchester City against Chelsea was a great experience, but we left at 5-1 down and got back on the coach so missed the last three City goals!

Generally, we supported him when we could, but we all had our own lives to lead. His fame certainly did not change us. These days with the money he could have earned he would have probably bought us all huge houses!

I used to organise football trips to Pontins at Prestatyn with Terry Lynch. I remember Eric turning up once when he was a City player. A guy asked if he could spend some time with the kids. For the next four hours all I can remember is Eric dressed in a crocodile suit with about 20 kids chasing him round and trying to stamp on his tail! He signed autographs for them all at the end. That is the way he was.

Barrie White

Wirral-based sports reporter

I always remember Eric as a superb kicker of the ball who always liked to get it moving forward. Despite his large frame, he was excellent at making saves low down. He watched a lot of local football and got to know a lot of the fans personally. If people came to talk to him he would chat back. There was never any arrogance about him. I read his column in the 'Echo'. He always talked a lot of good sense.

CAREER DETAILS

First-team appearances
(in chronological order – figures in brackets represent games as substitute)

CLUB	*Lge*	*FAC*	*LC*	*Other*	*Total*
Manchester City	58	10	8	8	84
Wolverhampton Wanderers	16	0	0	0	16
Bradford City	3	0	0	0	3
Southampton	4	0	0	0	4
Carlisle United	16	0	0	0	16
Tranmere Rovers	342 (4)	19	34 (1)	45 (1)	440 (6)
Reading	0	0	1	0	1
Blackpool	20	0	0	2	22
Bradford City	12	0	0	0	12
Stockport County	42	2	2	0	46
Wigan Athletic	3	0	0	0	3
Kidderminster Harriers	2	0	0	1	3
Sheffield Wednesday	0 (1)	0	0	0	0 (1)
TOTAL	518 (5)	31	45 (1)	56 (1)	650 (7)

Key:
FAC – FA Cup LC – League Cup Other – Includes Play-off games

CAREER LANDMARKS

10th December 1983

A spur-of-the-moment visit to Manchester City's Maine Road stadium to ask for a trial pays dividends. Eric makes enough of a positive impression to sign for his boyhood favourites for a transfer fee of £1,000 from non-League Curzon Ashton.

21st September 1985

Makes professional first-team debut,
Manchester City v West Ham United, Division One (2-2).

1985/86

Plays at Wembley Stadium for the first time, in the Full Members Cup final v Chelsea (4-5).

1986/87

Becomes the first player to play in all four divisions in the Football League in one season, having gone out on loan –

and played – for four clubs, as well as Manchester City: Southampton (Division One), Bradford City (Division Two), Carlisle United (Division Three) and Wolverhampton Wanderers (Division Four).

1987/88

Joins Tranmere Rovers for the first time, on loan. Saves a penalty at Wembley Stadium against First Division Newcastle United as he helps the unfancied side from the fourth tier reach the semi-finals of the Football League Centenary Trophy.

26th July 1988

Becomes Tranmere Rovers' record signing at £60,000.

1988/89

Helps Tranmere Rovers finish as Division Four runners-up, achieving the club's first promotion for 13 years.
Named in the PFA's Fourth Division Team of the Year (alongside team-mates Jim Harvey and Ian Muir).
Keeps a club record 25 clean sheets.

1989/90

Leyland DAF Cup winner v Bristol Rovers (2-1), which sees Tranmere Rovers achieve a first trophy success since winning Division Three North in 1937/38.
Helps the club finish fourth in Division Three, before being defeated in the play-off final v Notts County (0-2).
Named in PFA Third Division Team of the Year (alongside Jim Harvey and Ian Muir).

1990/91

Beaten in Leyland DAF Cup final v Birmingham City (2-3).
Promoted to Division Two as play-off winners v Bolton

Wanderers (1-0), having finished fifth in the league. It was the club's fourth appearance at Wembley in a 12-month period. Named in PFA Third Division Team of the Year (alongside team-mate Neil McNab).

1992

Receives the Dixie Dean Memorial award for services to football on Merseyside.

1992/93

Tranmere finish 4th in Division One, the highest position in the club's history. Rovers go on to lose in the play-off semi-finals 5-4 on aggregate to eventual winners Swindon Town.

1993/94

Helps Tranmere reach the League Cup semi-finals for the first time, where they are beaten on penalties by Premier League Aston Villa after the two-legged tie finished 4-4 on aggregate. Defeated by eventual winners Leicester City 2-1 on aggregate in the Division One play-off semi-finals, having finished fifth.

1994/95

Beaten in the Division One play-off semi-finals, this time 3-1 on aggregate by Reading, having again finished fifth.

27th August 1997

Ends 11-year stay at Prenton Park, signing for Stockport County for £100,000. He would return two years later.

21st September 2002

Becomes Tranmere's oldest player in making final appearance for the club, age 39 years and 352 days, as a substitute for Keith Welch at Crewe Alexandra (0-2).

27th September 2003
Final first-team appearance, coming on for Kevin Pressman in Sheffield Wednesday's 0-0 draw v Grimsby Town.

February 2007
Receives Dave Russell award for outstanding service to Tranmere Rovers.

References:
'Manchester City : The Complete Record' by Gary James (Breedon Books); 'Tranmere Rovers : The Complete Record' by Gilbert Upton, Steve Wilson and Peter Bishop (Breedon Books).

Other books from Sport Media

ALAN HANSEN'S STRANGEST FOOTBALL INJURIES

Hilarious collection of the most bizarre football injuries of all time

ALRIGHT ALDO: SOUND AS A POUND

Striking ace John Aldridge takes you on a road trip as he follows the fortunes of his former clubs, including Tranmere Rovers

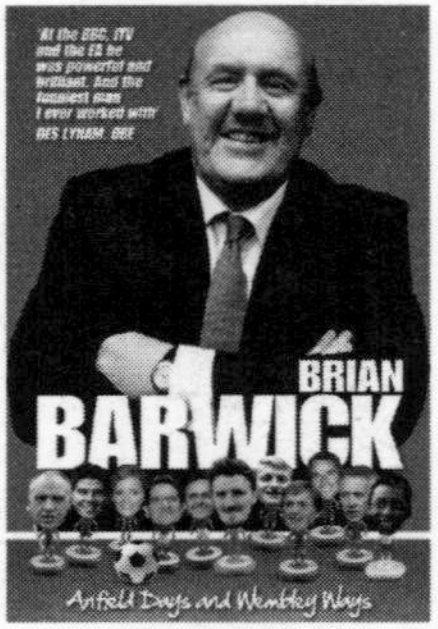

ANFIELD DAYS AND WEMBLEY WAYS

Insight into the life of former FA chief executive Brian Barwick

DODGY FOOTBALL FASHION

An amusing look at the best of the worst clothing crimes from some of the biggest names in football

All of these titles, and more, are available in print or e-book format. Order by calling 0845 143 0001, or online at www.merseyshop.com

Other books from Sport Media

PEPE: MY AUTOBIOGRAPHY

Liverpool and Spain's World Cup-winning goalkeeper talks candidly with Tony Barrett

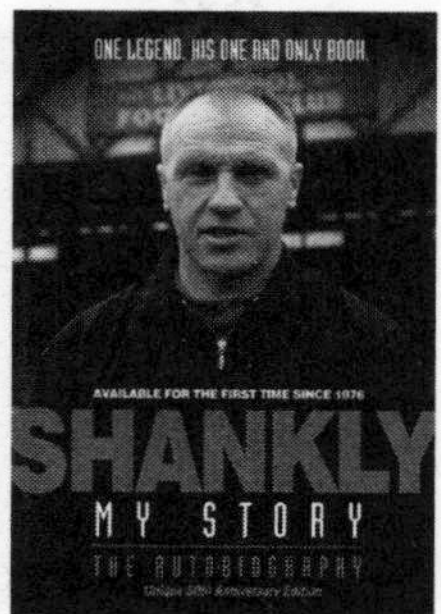

SHANKLY: MY STORY

The one and only autobiography of the legendary Liverpool manager

SNOD THIS FOR A LAUGH

A popular figure on both sides of the Pennines, Ian Snodin's on and off pitch life is rich in humour

SECRET DIARY OF A LIVERPOOL SCOUT

Story of Shankly's chief scout Geoff Twentyman, and the stars he discovered

All of these titles, and more, are available in print or e-book format. Order by calling 0845 143 0001, or online at www.merseyshop.com

Big Hands Big Heart

Sport Media